Social Skills Activities for the Elementary Grades

Dianne Schilling

Susanna Palomares

Mary Cook

Copyright © 1997, INNERCHOICE PUBLISHING • All rights reserved

ISBN 1-56499-036-2

Student experience sheets may be reproduced in quantities sufficient for distribution to students in groups utilizing *Social Skills Activities for the Elementary Grades*. All other reproduction for any purpose whatsoever is explicitly prohibited without written permission. Requests for permission may be directed to INNERCHOICE PUBLISHING.

INNERCHOICE PUBLISHING
P.O. Box 1185
Torrance, Ca 90505
Ph.-310-816-3085
E-mail-JalmarPress@att.net
http://www.jalmarpress.com

Contents

Introduction 1
Leading Sharing Circles 3
Activity Units
    Managing Anger and Fear 10
    Positive Self-talk 18
    Making Positive Choices 26
    Communicating Effectively 35
    Being Responsible 45
    Following Rules 53
    Understanding Body Language 60
    Making and Keeping Friends 70
    Cooperating With Others 77
    Helping Others 85
    Appreciating Differences 95
    Managing Conflict 104

SOCIAL SKILLS ACTIVITIES FOR THE ELEMENTARY GRADES: Contents

Introduction

Relating effectively to others is a challenge we all face. People who are effective in their social interactions have the ability to understand others. They know how to interact flexibly, skillfully, and responsibly. At the same time, they recognize their own needs and maintain their own integrity. Socially effective people can process the nonverbal as well as verbal messages of others. They possess the very important awareness that all people have the power to affect one another. They are aware of not only how others affect them, but the effects their behaviors have on others.

In order to build healthy relationships, children need to have positive interpersonal experiences and to gain information concerning the social realm of life. As a rule, we do not systematically teach children how to understand and get along with other people. However, since social skills are fundamental to success in life, and are learned behaviors, children should be consistently and developmentally taught these important skills.

It is important to recognize that people who enjoy effective social relationships are exhibiting not just one ability, but many different skills, each at a different level of development with different nuances of understanding.

The activities and Sharing Circles in this book are designed to help children become aware of the importance of effectively relating to others, and to teach them social interaction skills in a deliberate and enjoyable fashion. Each of the twelve instructional units addresses a specific area of skill development. Initial units focus on self-awareness, which is fundamental to understanding and relating well to others.

Each unit contains two Sharing Circles, this book's primary vehicle for teaching social skills to children. In addition, group activities provide children with experiences that allow them to explore interpersonal relations from many angles and through many learning styles. Discussion questions are an integral part of each activity, and encourage children to consider and internalize what they have learned.

How Sharing Circles Teach Social Skills

The Sharing Circle process has been designed so that healthy responsible behaviors are modeled by the teacher or counselor in his or her role as circle leader. The rules also require that the children relate positively and effectively to one another. The Sharing Circle brings out and affirms the positive qualities inherent in everyone and allows children to practice effective modes of communication. Through regular practice and reinforcement, children internalize effective interpersonal skills and are then able to transfer those skills to other situations. Because Sharing Circles provide a place where precipitants are listened to and their feelings accepted, children learn how to provide the same conditions to peers and adults outside the circle.

One of the great benefits of the Sharing Circle is that it does not merely teach young people about social interaction, it lets them interact! Every Sharing Circle is a real-life experience of social interaction where the children share, listen, explore, plan, dream, and problem solve together. As they interact, they learn about each other and they realize what it takes to relate effectively to others. Any given Sharing Circle may provide a dozen tiny flashes of positive interpersonal insight for an individual participant. Gradually, the reality of what constitutes effective behavior in relating to others is internalized.

Through this regular sharing of interpersonal experiences, the children learn that behavior can be positive or negative, and sometimes both at the same time. Consequences can be constructive, destructive, or both. Different people respond differently to the same event. They have different feelings and thoughts. The children begin to understand what will cause what to happen; they grasp the concept of cause and effect; they see themselves affecting others and being affected by others.

The ability to make accurate interpretations and responses in social interactions, when combined with growing self-knowledge and awareness, produces a broad and practical sense of values or ethics. When children possess this ability, they know where they stand with themselves and with others. They can tell what actions "fit" a situation. Sharing Circles are marvelous testing grounds where children can observe themselves and others in action, and can begin to see themselves as contributing to the good and bad feelings of others. With this understanding, children are helped to conclude that being responsible towards others feels good, and is the most valuable and personally rewarding form of interaction.

Leading Sharing Circles

The Sharing Circle is an organized discussion format that encourages spontaneous sharing in response to an assigned topic. The Sharing Circle is somewhat formal, and follows the same process and set of rules each time it occurs. However, no two Sharing Circles are the same—because the topics change, and because every participant brings a different set of views and experiences to the group. The Sharing Circle allows children the opportunity to explore aspects of human life with one another, to appreciate themselves and others as developing persons, to practice effective communication skills, and to develop empathy for and understanding of others.

The Sharing Circle's overall objectives are to increase children's self understanding, self-esteem, and sense of social skills. Several approaches are used to achieve these objectives. They include: The use of a circular, small-group seating arrangement; ground rules that set the tone for personal privacy and safety; and a procedural structure that invites each child to share, to give and receive reflective feedback, and to cognitively summarize the learnings that he or she has gained.

Does all of this mean that leading Sharing Circles is difficult? No. Sharing Circle leadership skills are quite simple. As a Sharing Circle leader, you will: follow a few simple steps as outlined below; state and enforce simple rules of considerate conduct; model your own respect for those rules; lead a discussion; verbally communicate with children in clear, non-patronizing language; and listen carefully (and respond appropriately) to what the children say. When you lead a Sharing Circle you are a teacher, model, coach, and co-participant all at the same time.

The Steps in Leading The Sharing Circle Are:

1. Set the tone.
2. Review the Sharing Circle Rules.
3. State the topic.
4. Give each child who volunteers a turn.
5. Conduct a review (optional).
6. Lead the summary.
7. Close the circle.

The following is an explanation of each step:

1. Set the Tone —
approximately 1 minute

Draw the children into the circle. Encourage them to make it perfectly circular so everyone will be able to see everyone else. Communicate welcome to the children. Through your eye contact, smile, gestures, etc., let the children know each one of them *belongs* in the group, and that you are looking forward to hearing what they have to say. Your enthusiastic, yet serious, attitude at this point says to the children: *This is an important time. We are going to learn about ourselves and each other. It's going to be interesting and fun.*

2. Review the Rules —
approximately 1-2 minutes

The Sharing Circle Rules:
- We bring ourselves to the circle and nothing else.
- Everyone gets one turn to share including the leader.
- We don't have to take a turn if we don't want to.
- We share the time equally.
- We listen to the person who is speaking.
- We stay in our own space, and we don't bother others with our hands or feet.
- We won't gossip, interrupt, or put each other down.

Rules are an extremely important part of the Sharing Circle because they clarify appropriate and inappropriate behaviors. Because of the universal nature of the Sharing Circle Rules, learning them not only equips a child for effective participation in the circle, but in many other life situations, as well. The rules of the Sharing Circle are teaching appropriate and effective social skills that can be transferred to any life endeavor that involves interaction with others. *These rules are fully explained later in this section.*

In your first few Sharing Circles, tell the children the rules and discuss them briefly. In subsequent sessions, ask the children to see how many of the rules they can remember—or ask individual children to tell the group which rule they particularly appreciate. As the children gradually demonstrate through their behavior that they understand the rules, dispense with these discussions, except for occasional reviews on an as-needed basis.

In addition to discussing the rules at the beginning of each Sharing Circle session, enforce them—just as you enforce other rules.

3. State the Topic — *approximately 1 minute*

When stating a topic, think of the process as having these four parts:
  A. State it.
  B. Elaborate.
  C. Restate it.
  D. Provide silent time for thinking.

Suggestions for introducing the Sharing Circle are written in each Sharing Circle topic activity in this book; however, since you know best how to communicate to your particular group of children, consider stating the introduction in your own words.

The goal in stating the topic is to clarify for the children what the Sharing Circle

session is about and what is expected of them if they decide to share. Therefore, when you elaborate, speak to the children in their own language, to the extent that you can do so without sounding phoney, simplistic, or patronizing. The intention is to eliminate confusion and assure the children that they can succeed if they volunteer to take a turn.

Providing silence for thinking gives the children a chance to decide *if* and *what* they want to share. It also has the effect of adding a note of relaxation to the session. At the end of the silent-thinking time, most children are centered and ready to share and listen.

No matter how tempted you might be to change to another topic (if the one you have offered doesn't seem to be going over well), we recommend you not do it. Although some topics are more challenging than others, and some are more fun than others, each topic relates to some aspect of life and is worthy of attention. If you expect the children to respond, they generally will. But if you keep changing the topic, you are, in effect, saying, *I'm going to keep on trying until I get you to say something.* This is a form of manipulation—and violates the rule assuring each child the right to participate simply by listening.

4. Give Each Child Who Volunteers a Turn — *approximately 1 minute per child*

Generally known as the "participation phase" of the Sharing Circle, this period of time is devoted to allowing each child, and you, to take one turn to respond to the topic. This is the time when circle members tell each other about their experiences, thoughts, and feelings in an atmosphere of acceptance and support.

It is most important that this portion of the circle be completely free of judgment, advice, or any other sort of distracting or negating commentary—even when the children copy each other's responses or state fabrications of reality.

During this time, give each child who wishes to respond the chance to do so. Assist individual children to make their contributions successfully by asking open-ended questions—but *only* if absolutely necessary. The less probing during this phase, the better. As each child takes a turn, model adherence to the Sharing Circle Rules, and enforce the rules, as necessary. As each child completes a turn, thank him or her for participating.

5. Conduct a Review (optional) — *approximately 30 seconds per circle member*

This is the only optional phase of the Sharing Circle and, as such, is offered at your discretion. Sometimes you will have time for it and the group's attention will be optimum. At other times, you may deem it undesirable.

The review phase of the Sharing Circle occurs right after the participation phase. Every circle member who wished to contribute has had a turn. The review simply offers the children who contributed a chance to hear other circle members tell them what they heard them share. *A review is a simple reflection and that is all.*

The purpose of the review is threefold: (1) to sharpen listening and observation skills, (2) to give circle members another chance to participate verbally, and (3) to assure children who spoke during the participation phase that they were

listened to. When we are listened to carefully, we feel valued. And when we find out that what we heard and saw was accurate, we feel confirmed. Thus, the first and second purposes relate to the development of effective communication, and the third purpose relates to the development of self-esteem.

The review is *not* an interpretation, an evaluation, or a chance for the reviewer to tell his or her own related story. None of these approaches enhances the self-esteem of the individual who is being reviewed to. In fact, they are often deflating. They are also time consuming.

Initiate a review by saying: *Let's review what we heard each other say. I'm going to pick Susan and review to her. Susan, you told us about...(brief summary of Susan's remarks). Did I hear you right?* Then ask a volunteer to review what another person said. Proceed in this manner until *every* circle member who took a turn during the participation phase is reviewed to, including you.

6. *Lead a Summary — approximately 1-3 minutes*

The summary is the cognitive portion of the Sharing Circle. During this phase, the leader asks thought-provoking questions to stimulate free discussion. Each Sharing Circle in this book includes two or more summary questions; however, at times you may want to formulate questions that are more appropriate to the level of understanding in your group.

The summary meets the need of people of all ages to find meaning in what they do. Thus, the summary serves as a necessary culmination to each Sharing Circle by allowing the children to clarify the key concepts they gained from the session.

7. *Close the Circle*

Due to its formal nature, the Sharing Circle should never be left without official closure. Thank the children for their cooperation and announce that the circle is over. You might also wish to announce the topic for the next circle, and tell the children when it will be held.

Review of the Sharing Circle Rules

The following is a detailed explanation of each of the Sharing circle rules:

The Sharing Circle Rules
- We bring ourselves to the circle and nothing else.
- Everyone gets one turn to share including the leader.
- We don't have to take a turn if we don't want to.
- We share the time equally.
- We listen to the person who is speaking.
- We stay in our own space, and we don't bother others with our hands or feet.
- We won't gossip, interrupt, or put each other down.

We bring ourselves to the circle and nothing else.

This rule helps the children realize that their *presence* in the Sharing Circle is the most important thing they can contribute. Therefore, just bringing themselves to the circle is all that's necessary.

This rule also lets the children know that material objects should not brought to the circle. When this rule is honored, distractions are minimized. The children are free to focus their attention on you and each other, instead of on objects in their hands. Whenever children do bring objects to the circle, gently ask them to place the objects under their chairs—or behind them, if they are seated on the floor.

Everyone gets one turn to share.

This rule let's the children state their knowledge that they will be included. Everyone will be given a turn—an equal opportunity to participate—because every individual is just as important as every other individual.

The word, "one" is also very important. When children are allowed more than one turn in the Sharing Circle, the session becomes difficult to manage, and the tone of equality is sacrificed. Children who enjoy talking and performing may vie with each other to gain your permission for additional turns. Such children tend to take up the allotted time with as many turns as they can obtain, causing reviews and summaries at the end of sessions to receive less time and attention.

Sometimes more outspoken children attempt to influence more reserved or reticent children to give them *their* turns, with the result that some children have no turn and others have numerous ones. With the allotment of *one* turn to share, the more outspoken children gradually realize that they need to mentally organize what they have to say before speaking. At the same time, the less outspoken children gradually realize that they are just as important as their more gregarious peers, and their contributions are just as valuable.

It is also important for the leader to take a turn. Creating a dialogue between the children and the teacher or counselor is vital. When children are able to participate with a teacher or counselor in this manner, bonding takes place. When you share with the children, you become a participant and they begin to see you as a *person* like themselves as well as their *teacher/counselor*.

We don't have to take a turn if we don't want to.

This rule allows the children to state their understanding that they will not be pressured to speak in the Sharing Circle. Because each circle member is valued for simply being present, and because each individual's privacy is honored, the decision to share is a matter of individual choice. A child may volunteer to speak to a topic, or not.

The most effective way to enforce this rule is to model it. Allow the children to volunteer to take turns during the Sharing Circle. Suggest that they raise their hands when they are ready to contribute, and then call on them. If some children have not raised their hands after all of the others have shared, yet look eager to participate, gently invite them to take a turn: *Sally, do you have something you'd like to say?* If the child demurs, treat the response with the same acceptance you show a child who shares. If the children pressure each other to speak, respectfully remind them of this rule.

We share the time equally.

This rule is closely related to the rule allowing everyone to have one turn. When a child is allowed to monopolize the time provided for the circle session, other children may not have enough time to participate, or reviews and summaries at the end of the session may suffer.

By controlling the amount of time taken by children who enjoy speaking, those children who are less outspoken will come to realize the value of the time they have been given and to realize that what they are contributing is valued and valuable.

We listen to the person who is speaking.

By stating this rule, the children remind themselves that each person will receive everyone's attention when he or she is taking a turn. And that *you* will receive attention when you are clarifying the topic, leading the review, or asking summary questions.

The most effective way to teach children to give their attention to the person who is speaking is to model this behavior yourself. If some of the children are not listening, encourage them to do so by acknowledging those children who *are* giving the speaker their attention: *Good for you, Dave. I noticed how you looked right at Judy and listened to her as she spoke.* As soon as a child listens who has previously had difficulty doing so, be sure to reinforce him or her.

NOTE: The optional review portion of the Sharing Circle (step 5) is included because it sharpens children's listening skills. In fact, the reason it is optional is that, occurring intermittently as it does, the review holds more power to encourage effective listening than it would if it occurred as a feature of every session.

We stay in our own space and we don't bother others with our hands or feet.

When the children state this rule, they are recognizing the importance of respecting each individual's physical space. This is a very important ground rule, because, when followed, it prevents the major distractions that result from annoying body contact. Distractions of this nature disrupt the flow of the Sharing Circle, make it difficult to give attention to the person who is sharing, and result in less enjoyment for everyone.

Try to prevent space violations by separating troublesome pairs when the group sits down, or by placing yourself between them. Praise the children when they follow the rule by saying, for example: *I'm very impressed with how you are all staying in your own spaces today. This way we can have a fine Sharing Circle.*

At times, one child will blatantly poke or kick another. When this occurs, remind the child of the rule. If the child persists, remind him/her again. As a last resort ask the child to leave the circle. However, if you can, continue the session with the offending child present, perhaps having him/her change places with another child. Then speak to the child privately after the circle. *Chris, I need your help. I want to have good Sharing Circles, but it's hard when you keep poking the person next to you. Everyone looks at you and forgets what we're doing. I want you to stay in the Sharing Circle because we get to know you better when you are with us. But we can't have you there if you keep poking other children. Will you help?* If

SOCIAL SKILLS ACTIVITIES FOR THE ELEMENTARY GRADES: Leading Sharing Circles

the child persists, give him or her something less desirable to do during the next Sharing Circle and explain why you are excluding him/her. After the session, approach the child and say that you missed him/her, and invite the child to come to the next session; however, caution the child not to bother other children.

G. We won't, gossip, interrupt, or put down each other.

This is another very important rule. Like annoying physical contact, interruptions and put downs are very distracting and disruptive to the Sharing Circle. They are capable of changing a supportive, enjoyable atmosphere to one of confusion and disharmony.

By stating this rule, the children are taking the first step to preventing the damage that interruptions and put downs can cause. Your careful modeling also has a powerful influence on the children. When you demonstrate to every child *your own* attention, acceptance, appreciation, and affection, your behavior sets the tone, and is likely to be imitated by the children.

Acknowledge the children when they honor this ground rule. Say: *I've noticed something. No one has interrupted anyone else during this session. Isn't that great?*

If a child does interrupt, or put another down, determine his conscious or unconscious motive before you decide what to do. If the action was designed to gain attention, reward it with as little attention as possible. Tell the child: *Johnny is speaking, Susan. Remember the promise not to interrupt?* or *Please don't say things like that, Wally. That's a put down and it can make Jerome feel bad about you.* Deliver these words in a cool tone, with low energy and minimal eye contact. Another alternative is to simply touch the child firmly on the knee or shoulder, with no eye contact at all.

If gaining attention is not the child's motive for interrupting or putting another down, deliver these same words in a more energetic (perhaps even warm) manner. The child may simply want to make contact with the individual he or she has interrupted (or put down), and may have seen other people use similar methods to make interpersonal contact.

Summary

The Sharing Circle process and topics teach and reinforce positive social skills. Through regular participation, children learn to listen and to speak effectively. They learn self-control by waiting to take their turn to speak, and they learn to pay attention to others. The optional review requires that the children listen and remember what other children are saying. Through a variety of topics, both positive and negative, children learn to recognize, value and respect the similarities and differences between people. Relating effectively to others requires that children acquire these basic understandings; appreciation and empathy for others develop from them.

Children learn about what works and what doesn't work in social relationships through verbally exploring their own experiences and listening to the experiences of others. The circle process creates a safe, nonthreatening vehicle through which this awareness develops and grows.

Managing Anger And Fear

We all experience anger and fear, and most of us have trouble dealing with these feelings at times. People who experience a great deal of trouble with anger and fear sometimes have poor relations with others because of this. This unit is designed to help children better understand these difficult emotions, and to develop positive strategies for handling them. It will also help them distinguish between those fears that are real and those that are imagined, and utilize creativity in deciding how they will respond to feelings of anger and fear.

Something That Really Makes Me Angry

A Sharing Circle

Directions:

Introduce the topic: *Our topic for this session is, "Something That Really Made Me Angry.*

Elaborate: *Think of a time something made you angry—a time that you'd feel OK telling us about. It could be a time when someone treated you unfairly, or a time that you were angry with yourself for breaking or losing something you liked. Or perhaps you were mad because you couldn't do something you wanted to do. It can be anything big or small that made you mad. Let's take a few quiet moments to think it over. The topic is, "Something That Really Made Me Angry."*

Invite the children to take turns sharing. Listen carefully to each one and encourage the other children to do the same. Don't allow negative interruptions. Be sure to take a turn yourself.

Discussion Questions:

After each child who wants to speak has done so, ask the children:
— *How do our bodies react when we are angry?*
— *What are some things we can do when we are angry to change how we are feeling?*

A Time I Was Scared

A Sharing Circle

Directions:

Introduce the topic: *Our topic for this session is, "A Time I Was Scared."*

Elaborate: *Lots of things can be scary to all of us. Think of something that scared you. Perhaps you were at home alone and heard noises, or maybe you were afraid that you wouldn't be included in some activity or event. It might have been that you wanted to do something really well and were afraid you would fail—by striking out when someone was in scoring position, or by letting someone down who was counting on you. Take a few silent moments to think it over, and remember, "A Time I Was Scared."*

Invite the children to take turns speaking. Listen carefully to each one and encourage the other children to do the same. Don't allow negative interruptions. Be sure to take a turn yourself.

Discussion Questions:

After each child who wants to speak has done so, ask the children:
— What similarities and differences did you notice in the fears we shared?
— What are some ways we could lessen our fears or even make them disappear?

I Can See It All Now

Relaxation Activity

Materials:

Optional cassette tape player and tape of relaxing instrumental music.

Directions:

If you have music, start the tape at a low volume so you can speak over it easily. Make your voice loud enough to be heard, but soft enough to be relaxing. Read the following passage slowly, pausing when you see two dots (. .) so the children have ample time to picture things in their minds as you read.

Explain: *You are going to use your mind to take an imaginary trip. Sit in a comfortable position with your eyes closed so that you can imagine things as I talk to you. Make sure you are not touching your neighbor. Uncross you arms and legs, close your eyes, and take a deep breath. Slowly let it out like this. (Demonstrate this.) Now you do it. Breathe in and let it out. Again. (Continue to breathe in and out with them three to five times.) As you relax . . and take in one more full, deep breath . . and exhale . . excellent . . relax . . Allow your imagination to help you recall a time you were angry. . It may have occurred recently or a long time ago . . a time when you were angry and upset . . Put yourself in that moment . .What do you see?. .What do you hear?. . Can you remember what you said?. . What was it?. . Is there shouting?. . or silence?. . What did you do?. . Did you hit? run?. . break something?. . say things you wish you hadn't?. . Now think of how you wish you had acted . . Could you hit a pillow instead of someone? . . or talk to a friend? . . or write your feelings out? . . exercise? . . Picture the perfect way for you to react to this situation . .What can you say? . . What can you do differently than before? . . See yourself saying exactly the right thing at the*

Continued on Next Page . . .

I Can See It All Now

Relaxation

(Continued)

right time . . Tell yourself, "I have wonderful self-control" . . "I know many positive ways to handle anger" . . good . . And now, as you gradually shift back to the present moment, allow those positive feelings and ideas to stay with you . . You can call upon these skills any time you choose . . Notice that your breathing is becoming stronger as you gently open your eyes, feeling perfect in every way.

If you're using music, keep it playing. The children may want to stretch.

Discussion Questions:

Ask if anyone would like to share how he or she turned anger into a positive action. Thank those who choose to share. If no one shares, simply tell the children that the imagining technique will work for them anytime and they can use it to help deal with anger situations.

Other things To Try:

A similar relaxation activity can be done using fear as the area to be managed.

Actions Speak Louder Than Words

Brainstorming and Pantomime

Materials:

Chart paper and magic marker or chalkboard and chalk, slips of paper, and a box, jar, or other container to hold the slips of paper.

Directions:

Gather the children together and ask: *Have you ever heard someone say, "I'm fine," and known that he or she was mad or sad or something other than "fine?" Our bodies and facial expressions almost always reveal what we are feeling, even if it's not the same as what we are saying.*

Brainstorm: Ask the children to name as many words as they can that mean some level of angry. From low levels of angry, like *irritate* and *annoy*, all the way up to high levels, like *furious* and *enraged*. Record their list on chart paper. Leave the chart in place while you copy the words on slips of paper. Place the slips in a container. Have each child draw one slip of paper and pantomime the word. The children can use facial expressions, gestures, and body language, but may *not* say any words. Have the group guess which word (from the chart) is being acted out. Whoever guesses correctly gets to be the next person to draw a word and act it out.

Other Things To Try:

The children can do a similar activity with partners. One child acts out one of the anger words and the partner pantomimes a positive emotion or feeling. With this variation, a list of positive words would need to be brainstormed along with the anger words. Pairs of words (one from each list) would be placed in the container.

That's What Scares Me

Art Activity

Materials:

Paper, crayons, magic markers, and/or chalk in lots of colors.

Directions:

Distribute the materials. Tell the children that they will have a chance to draw something that scares them and then get rid of the thing that scares them in a second drawing.

Explain: *We've all had bad dreams or nightmares. Think of a bad dream you have had and draw a picture of it. Put all the things in it that you can remember, especially the scary part. Then on another piece of paper, draw a picture of the same situation, but draw it so it's not scary anymore. After we finish the drawings, we'll talk about them.*

Demonstrate by drawing a picture of a nightmare that *you* had as a child, and then redraw it to place yourself in control.

As the children work, offer suggestions to those who are having difficulty, but let them work independently.

Discussion: As they draw, praise and encourage the children for their ideas, rather than for the quality of their drawings. Ask volunteers to describe what is happening in their pictures—first the scary parts, and then how they redrew the pictures so they wouldn't have to be afraid anymore. Thank each volunteer.

Other Things To Try:

Have each child draw a picture of a scary nightmare and share it with the group. Then have the group brainstorm ways to change the picture to get rid of the scary parts.

F E A R = False Evidence Appearing Real

Experience Sheet

Think about times when you were afraid of someone or something and everything turned out OK. There was nothing to fear after all. It was only "false evidence appearing real." Make a list:

FEAR: **WHAT REALLY HAPPENED:**

Example: Thought I'd failed the test   I got a B–

_____   _____

_____   _____

_____   _____

_____   _____

Can you think of a time when you got mad at someone else, but once you understood their point of view, you found you really didn't have so much to be angry about? Tell that story here:

_____

_____

_____

_____

_____

_____

Positive Self-talk

As we respond to the people and events in our lives, we hear our own voices. Unfortunately, too much of what we hear is negative and discouraging. Since positive self-esteem is built with an "I can" attitude, and since positive attitudes and esteem are indicators of how well people get along with and understand others, it is important that the messages we give ourselves be encouraging—not discouraging. The more children can learn to be their own encouragers, the greater their chances for success in all areas. This unit offers children a variety of opportunities to transform negative self-talk to positive self-talk, and to consciously give themselves encouraging words.

A Time I Knew I Could Do It

A Sharing Circle

Directions:

Introduce the topic: *Our topic for this session is, "A Time I Knew I Could Do It."*

Elaborate: *Sometimes we just know we can do something. We don't doubt it at all. Think of a time when you felt confident that you could do something. It might have been that you knew you could master a new dance step, pass a test, sink a basket, or get your room clean before you went to the movies. It could have been something quick and easy that required limited effort, or something more difficult. Whatever it was, you knew you could do it—and you were right. Take a few moments to think it over, and remember, "A Time I Knew I Could Do It."*

You might want to share first this time. Then invite the children to take turns speaking. Listen carefully, and thank each person for sharing. Don't allow negative interruptions.

Discussion Questions:

After each child who wants to speak has done so, ask the children:
— *How did you know that you could do the thing you shared?*
— *Do you think you could do the same thing again? Why or why not?*

I Succeeded Because I Encouraged Myself

A Sharing Circle

Directions:

Introduce the topic: *Our topic for this session is, "I Succeeded Because I Encouraged Myself."*

Elaborate: *Have you ever wanted to do something and weren't quite sure you could? Think of a time when you felt unsure, but encouraged yourself and, consequently, found a way to be successful. Perhaps you tried to teach your pet a trick, or needed to do a good job on a report for school. Maybe you were trying to master something on a computer, or were learning a new game. Whatever it was, you were not sure you could do it, but after giving yourself some encouraging words, you were successful. Take a few quiet moments to think it over. The topic is, "I Succeeded Because I Encouraged Myself."*

Invite the children to take turns speaking. Make sure there are no negative interruptions. Listen attentively and thank each child for sharing. Be sure to take a turn yourself.

Discussion Questions:

After every child who wants to speak has done so, ask the children:
— What do you think caused each of you to be successful?
— What kinds of doubts did you have to overcome to be successful?
— What do you think would have happened if you had used discouraging words instead of encouraging words?

No Time to Be Modest

Art Activity

Materials:

Poster paper and magic markers in various colors.

Directions:

Explain to the children that positive self-talk consists of encouraging words that we say to ourselves that help us succeed. (Remind them of the things they shared in the Sharing Circle, *I Succeeded Because I Encouraged Myself*.) Encouraging words are helpful and powerful, particularly when we put them into positive statements about ourselves. They are especially helpful when we are feeling discouraged, or have some negative feelings about being able to accomplish something.

Explain: *Think of three strong, positive statements about yourself, such as "I am a good athlete," "I am very smart," or "I am a great listener." Your statements should be about things that you want to <u>become</u> skillful at—rather than things you are <u>already</u> skillful at.*

Pass out the materials, and have the children write their statements in large letters on the poster paper. Tell them to use the magic markers to make their statements colorful and decorative. Prepare a statement yourself to show as an example. Tell the children to take their statements home and place them on a wall, or in another location where they will see them often. Tell them that each time they look at their statements, they will become more and more like them.

Discussion: While they work, talk to the children about encouraging words, and how they can help us become more positive and capable. Assist any children who get stuck, or inadvertently include something negative in their statements. Reinforce the children for the positive statements they make. Point out that although sometimes we're told it's impolite or conceited to say good things about ourselves, these encouraging statements are not like that. They are to help us do things we want to do.

Dear Me . . .

Letter-Writing Activity

Materials:

Writing paper and pens or pencils. One envelope and one first-class postage stamp per child.

Note: For maximum impact, do this activity *after* the children have completed the Experience Sheet, *Mirror, Mirror—What to Say to Yourself.*

Directions:

Tell the children that they are going to write a very special letter to themselves. They are to be exceedingly complimentary, and include all the encouraging words they can think of. The letter should contain only positive comments and remarks—nothing negative or discouraging. It should recognize their good traits, attributes, and accomplishments, and should inspire them to keep working on areas in which they want to improve. Set the tone by sharing several sample sentences with the children.

Pass out the materials. Tell the children to begin writing. When they are finished, have them address and stamp their envelopes. Collect the letters, and put them away in a safe place for three months. Then mail them to the students.

Discussion: While the children are busy writing, circulate and offer assistance. Remind the children of how important their words are, and how they are affected by them. Point out that since television, newspapers, and people seem to bombard us with negatives, at times, we need all the positive input we can get.

High on My Kite

Craft Activity

Materials:

Scissors, ruler, pencil, paste, 3/4-inch cellulose tape, glue, marking pens, and a sharp pocket knife. **For each kite:** white or brown wrapping paper; 300 feet of strong, soft white cotton household string; an empty plastic bottle or wide piece of wood for line reel; one 21-inch piece of split bamboo stake for the spar; and another 28-inch piece for the spine. **Optional:** cassette recorder with a tape of "Let's Go Fly a Kite" from the movie "Mary Poppins" (looped several times) to set the mood; for reference, library books on kite-building.

Directions:

Gather the children together and tell them that they are going to build tadpole kites. Have them choose partners. Urge the children to follow the directions precisely, and to be careful with the tools and materials. <u>Make your kite first, so you will be prepared to demonstrate each step of the kite building process.</u>

Give each child one 21-inch and one 28-inch stick, and tell them: *Find and mark the center of the short stick (spar). Measure and mark 7 inches from one end of the long stick (spine). Make a cross with the short stick centered 7 inches from the top of the long stick. Glue and bind the intersection. Then use a 10-foot long piece of string to frame the kite. Start with the notched end of one stick, and in sequence, attach the string to the remaining notched ends of both sticks. Be sure to keep the framing string taut, and maintain the cross (the intersection of the sticks) at right angles.*

Cut wrapping paper to cover the frame. Use the framed cross as a pattern. Allow the paper to extend 1 1/2 inches beyond the frame on all sides. Fold the extensions over the frame and paste. Cut a 40-inch string for the bridle (this holds the kite at the correct angle to the wind). Tie the ends of the bridle to the top and

Continued on Next Page . . .

High on My Kite

(Continued)

Craft Activity

bottom of the spine. Leave about 8 inches of slack in the bridle.

The paper tail (which keeps the tadpole kite upright) will need to be 4 to 7 times the length of the spine, depending on the wind strength. To make a banner tail, cut 35 triangular flags from 10-inch wide strips of wrapping paper. Using marking pens, write encouraging words or positive statements on each of the flags. Paste them to the tail string by folding the wide ends over the string. Place a piece of tape between each flag to prevent tearing.

Attach the free end of the string (for flying the kite) to the bridle. The initial attachment should be 8 inches from the top end of the bridle string. Sticky tape on either side of the attachment will keep the string from slipping.

Go fly the kites: Take the children and their kites out to the school playground. Select an area where the kites will be clear of power lines, trees, and people. A park, beach, or other open spot would also be an excellent place to fly the kites.

Special Instructions:

Carry a repair kit: Take a pocket knife, scissors, roll of sticky tape, paper for patching, and extra string. With a tadpole kite, it is important to have plenty of extra tail material in case the tail must be extended.

To launch the kite: Have the children stand with their backs to the wind, and hold their kites up to catch the wind. As the wind takes the kites up, tell the children to let out more line. To avoid painful cuts, caution the children not to let the line run too quickly through their fingers.

Adjusting the rigging: The stronger the wind, the longer the tail must be to keep it steady. Show the children

Continued on Next Page . . .

High on My Kite

Craft Activity

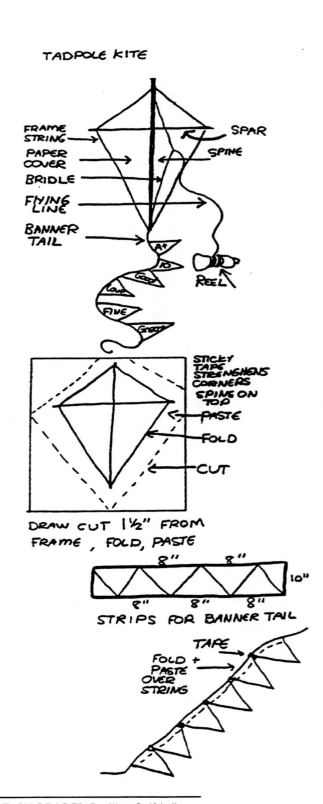

how to move the towing position up or down the bridle string to change the kite's angle of attack to the wind. The stronger the wind, the higher the towing position.

Discussion Questions:

After the kite fly, lead the children in a discussion concerning their efforts. Ask them:
— What did you enjoy most about this activity?
— Do you think that you could build another kite? How would you make the second kite better than the first one?
— What encouraging words did you say to yourself as you attempted to get your kite airborne?
— If your kite didn't fly or didn't fly very long, what kinds of things did you say to yourself?
— What encouraging words did you say to <u>others</u>?
— What connection is there between what you say to yourself and the kind of experience you have?

Mirror, Mirror — What to Say to Yourself

Experience Sheet

Sometimes other people say discouraging words to us. And sometimes, we say discouraging words to ourselves, too. When we listen to discouraging words, we begin to have doubts about ourselves. That's when we need help.

Try this:

On a separate piece of paper, write down 3 of the most negative things you've ever said to yourself—or that someone else has said to you.

Now rewrite those negative statements, so that they are positive and encouraging.
Example: *I'm just no good at math.*
Change to: *Math problems are easy and fun to solve.*

1. _____

2. _____

3. _____

Now try this:

Take the paper with the discouraging words on it, and shred it into bits. As you throw the bits of paper away, tell yourself that you are throwing away all those discouraging thought and beliefs. They are gone.

And this:

Sit in front of a mirror and repeat your positive statements aloud to yourself several times. Say them with great strength and feeling. Look yourself squarely in the eye as you speak. **Convince yourself that these things are true!**

Making Positive Choices

We are the products of the choices we make. When we learn this, and become conscious of our choice-making, and of the consequences of our choices, we can direct our lives onto positive and productive paths. The first step toward making wise choices is making positive ones! This unit provides children with experiences that allow them to become conscientious, productive choicemakers.

Something I Chose That Made Me Happy

A Sharing Circle

Directions:

Introduce the topic: *Our topic for this session is, "Something I Chose That Made Me Happy."*

Elaborate: *Think of a time when you had a choice to make. Maybe you had to choose something you wanted to do, or what clothes you wanted to wear, or a place you wanted to go. The choice could have involved something really special, or just something ordinary, but whatever it was, you were pleased with the results of your choice. Take a moment and think about it. The topic is, "Something I Chose that Made Me Happy."*

Invite the children to take turns sharing. Listen carefully to each one and, through your example, assist the other children to do the same. Don't allow negative interruptions. Be sure to take a turn yourself.

Discussion Questions:

When everyone in the circle has had a chance to speak, ask the children:
— *How many different kinds of choices do we make every day?*
— *What are some choices that might have made you unhappy in the situation you shared?*
— *Does thinking about being happy help us make good choices?*

A Hard Choice That I Had to Make

A Sharing Circle

Directions:

Introduce the topic: *Our topic for this session is, "A Hard Choice That I Had to Make."*

Elaborate: *Can you think of a choice that you didn't want to make, but had to make anyway? Maybe the choice involved something you had to tell someone, or an unpleasant job you had to do. Or perhaps you were going to put off doing something, but decided to go ahead and do it after all. Take some time and think about it. The topic is, "A Hard Choice That I Had to Make."*

Invite the children to take turns sharing. Listen to each one carefully and help the other children do the same. Don't allow negative interruptions. Be sure to take a turn yourself.

Discussion Questions:

After everyone in the circle has had a chance to share, ask the children:
— How did you feel when you remembered the hard choice that you made?
— Are there times when choosing isn't as hard as we think it will be? Why do you think that is?

What Do You Really, Really, Really Want

Art/Creative Thought

Materials:

Enough colored notebook-size paper so that each child has three sheets. White glue, scissors, pens or pencils, and plenty of magazines that children look at or read.

Directions:

Place the materials on large tables and divide them evenly among the children. The children will be cutting words and pictures from the magazines and gluing them to their sheets of colored paper. They can also *create* drawings and designs to supplement what they find in the magazines.

Explain: *We are going to make pictures of the things we really, really, really want to have in our lives. Take a moment and think about what you would like most to have, to be, to see, or to do. Now, make a list of the three most important things you want. Cut out pictures and words that describe what you want from the magazines, and glue them to your paper. You have one sheet on which to show each thing you want. If you like, make drawings and designs of your own.*

As the children work, watch to see if you can assist anyone who is having difficulty. Let them be as creative as they wish. There is no right or wrong way to do this activity; however, the wants that the children depict need to be positive. Allow enough time for work and cleanup.

Discussion: During the activity, assist where you can, and reassure the children that they are doing fine. Ask the children to talk about their choices, acknowledging each child with appreciation.

Other Things To Try:

Conduct a sharing session during which the children each display one of their sheets and talk about what they've chosen and why.

We Decided to Do It This Way

Group Choice and Presentation

Materials:

One hundred pennies, beans or some other item that can represent money for each group. Writing paper, and pens or pencils.

Directions:

Have the children form groups of four or six depending on the total number of children involved. Each group will receive one hundred pennies or beans, which will become that group's treasury. Together the children will cooperate to make choices about how best to use this treasury.

Explain: *Each group has been given one-hundred pennies or beans. Pretend that each penny or bean is a dollar, so that you really have one-hundred dollars. Working individually, I want you to think of the very best way to use your group's money. Then, when we're all ready, you'll work with the others in your group to make one choice from among all of your ideas about how to use the money. When your group has made its choice, write it down.*

Allow time for individual thought, and offer any help needed for the children to make their individual decisions. After several minutes, ask the groups to start making their group choices. Ask each group to indicate when it has completed the task. Don't proceed until all groups are finished.

During the activity you may want to offer some suggestions. When the groups have finished, ask each to present its choice. Be sure to acknowledge each group's efforts.

Continued on Next Page . . .

We Decided to Do It This Way

(Continued)

Group Choice and Presentation

Discussion Questions:

After all the groups have shared their choices, ask the children the following questions:
— Was it easy or difficult for you to make a choice on how you would spend the money for yourself?
— Was it easy or difficult for your group to make a joint decision on how to spend the money? What was the difference?
— What are some things that people can do when they have to make a group decision that will make the process easier for them?
— What did you learn from this activity about getting along with others?

SOCIAL SKILLS ACTIVITIES FOR THE ELEMENTARY GRADES: Making Positive Choices

Choose in the News

News Review and Discussion

Materials:

Current newspapers (one for every two children), scissors, writing paper, and pens or pencils.

Directions:

Organize the children into pairs, and give a newspaper and other materials to each pair. The children will be reviewing headlines and articles that show choices that people make, and the results or outcomes of those choices. They will cut out the articles they choose, and write down both the choice and the outcome described in each article.

Explain: *Work with your partner to find two articles in the newspaper. Look at the headlines. Pick one article in which a person, a group of people, or an organization made a choice that caused something good to happen. After that, find an article that describes a choice that caused something bad to happen. Cut out the articles, and write down the choice and outcome for each one.* As the children work, pass among them and give help, where needed.

Discussion Questions:

After all pairs have finished, ask the group, *What is the difference between a choice and an outcome, or result?* Now ask the children to share their articles and the choices and outcomes they recorded.

After the presentations, ask the group the following questions:
— In the articles with bad outcomes, what other choices could have been made?
— If another choice had been made, what might have been the outcome?

Other Things To Try:

Have the children write short newspaper articles about choices they have made, and the outcomes of their choices.

Choices I Made Today

Log Keeping and Discussion

Materials:

The Experience Sheet *If I Get To Choose . . . and I Do!* (one per child).

Directions:

Hand out the Experience Sheets and introduce this activity to the children by saying: *You may not think of it this way, but you are always making choices. With the help of your Experience Sheet you're going to look at the choices you make every day. Use your Experience Sheet to write a list of all the choices you make during a day.*

For the next twenty-four hours, every time you make a choice, write it down. After each choice, write the outcome. Sometimes outcomes happen right away, like choosing something to eat and having it taste good. Sometimes outcomes don't happen for awhile. For example, when you save money to buy something, the outcome doesn't happen until enough money is saved to buy the thing you want.

See how many choices and outcomes you can write down in a day.

Tomorrow, we'll talk about all the choices we made.

At the end of the day, remind the children to complete their lists and to be sure to bring them back to the next day's class.

Discussion Questions:

At the next meeting, have the children share some of the choices and outcomes they recorded. After all of the children who wish to have shared, spend time discussing their experiences. Ask them:
— *Did you make some choices without thinking?*
— *What were some big choices you made?*
— *What were some little choices you made?*
— *Do you think you wrote down all of the choices you made?*
— *What were some choices you made that had immediate outcomes?*
— *What were some choices whose outcomes won't happen for awhile?*
— *Were you surprised at how many choices you made?*

If I Get to Choose... and I Do!

Experience Sheet

For one entire day keep track of all the choices you make. Write about what each choice was and what the outcome was, or will probably be.

1. A choice I made: _____
   _____

   What happened because of the choice I made: _____
   _____

2. A choice I made: _____
   _____

   What happened because of the choice I made: _____
   _____

3. A choice I made: _____
   _____

   What happened because of the choice I made: _____
   _____

4. A choice I made: _____
   _____

   What happened because of the choice I made: _____
   _____

5. A choice I made: _____
   _____

   What happened because of the choice I made: _____
   _____

Use the back of your Experience Sheet or more paper if you need more room.

Communicating Effectively

Some of the most important skills we can learn are those that relate to effective communication. Individuals who consistently speak and listen accurately have greater control over themselves, and greater influence in dealing with others. This unit is designed to help the children focus on both the speaking and listening aspects of communication, identify ways in which they can improve their abilities in both areas, and develop a keener awareness of how important it is to communicate well.

Someone I Like to Talk With

A Sharing Circle

Directions:

Introduce the topic: *Our topic for this Sharing Circle is, "Someone I Like to Talk With."*

Elaborate: *Being able to talk with other people is very important for all of us. Most of us find that certain people we know are easier to talk with than others. Can you think of someone with whom you enjoy having conversations? Perhaps the person you like to talk with is a good friend your own age, or a teenager—or maybe he or she is an adult. Tell us about the person and what kind of conversations you have. Let's take a few silent moments to think it over. The topic is, "Someone I Like to Talk With."*

Invite the children to take turns speaking. Model good listening by showing the children what a good listener you are. Don't allow negative interruptions. Be sure to take a turn yourself.

Discussion Questions:

After each child who wants to speak has done so, ask the children:
— *Why are conversations with the people we talked about so satisfying?*
— *Do all of these people have similar qualities and abilities and, if so, what are they?"*
— *Is being able to speak well an important ability for each of us to develop? Why?*

SOCIAL SKILLS ACTIVITIES FOR THE ELEMENTARY GRADES: Communicating Effectively

A Time I Listened Well to Someone

A Sharing Circle

Directions:

Introduce the topic: *The topic for this session is, "A Time I Listened Well to Someone."*

Elaborate: *We've been doing a lot of talking and sharing in our Sharing Circles, and we have also been listening well to each other. If we hadn't been good listeners, our circles wouldn't have worked. Listening is just as important in communication as talking. Can you think of a time when you listened carefully to another person? Perhaps you had a friend who needed to talk about a problem, and you showed you cared by listening and saying very little. Or maybe it was a situation in which you learned a lot from someone who had some interesting and important things to say. Think about times like these, when you used your listening skills, and tell us about one of them. Let's take a few moments of silence to think it over. The topic is, "A Time I Listened Well to Someone."*

Invite the children to take turns speaking. Listen carefully to each one and guide the other children to do the same. Don't allow negative interruptions. Be sure to take a turn yourself.

Discussion Questions:

After each child who wants to speak has done so, ask the children:
— *Can you tell if someone is listening to you or not?*
— *When you know someone is listening, how does it make you feel?*
— *How do you feel when the person you are talking to isn't listening?*

Correct Cues Can Be Crucial

Practice in Precise Communication

You Will Need:

An outdoor or indoor area with numerous large objects, such as plants, furniture, trash cans, etc.

Directions:

Set up an obstacle course using the plants, furniture, trash cans, etc. This will be the "runway" over which the "pilots" in this activity must be guided.

Talk with the children about how important it is for people to communicate clearly and accurately. Ask them to imagine what would happen if airplane pilots didn't communicate clearly with air traffic controllers, or quarterbacks didn't communicate accurately with their football teams. Airplanes would crash, and football teams wouldn't be able to run their plays.

Blindfold one child and spin him or her around at one end of the runway. This person is the pilot. Station a second child at the other side of the runway—the pilot's destination. Announce that this person is the air traffic controller.

Explain: *When you are the air traffic controller, it is your job to guide the pilot (called "Captain") step-by-step through the obstacles using words only. If the pilot touches anything, it counts as a crash, and your turn is over. The pilot may direct questions to the air traffic controller. The rest of us will be very quiet during the exercise.*

Give everyone a chance to try both roles.

Discussion Questions:

After everyone has had a turn, ask the children:
— *What can we learn from this experiment?*
— *What are some examples of other situations in which it would be essential to communicate very clearly?*

Other Things To Try:

Ask a pilot, air traffic controller, or high school quarterback to visit the group. Encourage the children to ask questions about how the guest communicates precisely with others on the job. Urge the visitor to give a few examples of precise communication.

SOCIAL SKILLS ACTIVITIES FOR THE ELEMENTARY GRADES: Communicating Effectively

The Big Muddy

Group Experiment and Discussion

Directions:

Ask the children to sit down with you in a circle. Then explain: *This may seem like a Sharing Circle, but it's not. This is an experiment called, "The Big Muddy." I'm going to whisper something into the ear of the person on my right, and try not to let the rest of you hear what I say. Then he or she will whisper it into the ear of the person on her right, and he or she will do the same, until everyone has heard the message and whispered it to the next person. After the last person has heard the message, he or she will say it out loud. Then I will tell you what I said in the beginning. Let's do it and see what happens.*

Begin the experiment: As the message is whispered, encourage the children to be as quiet as possible, and to observe each whisperer and listener in turn. Ask the last person who hears the message to repeat it out loud. Then tell the group what you said to the first person when you started the experiment. The difference between the two messages will probably cause amazement and laughter.

Ask the children why they think the activity is called, "The Big Muddy." After they respond, suggest that they do the activity again, and ask a volunteer to start a new message.

As time allows, give as many children as possible an opportunity to start a message.

Discussion Questions:

Between messages, talk with the children about how communication can become muddy when it is passed from one person to another many times. When the activity is complete ask the following questions:
— Why do you think the first message is so different from the last message?
— How can poor communication cause misunderstandings between people or groups?
— What kind of similarities did you notice between what happened in the activity and gossip or rumors?
— What did you learn from this activity?

Tape the Message and Play It Back

Dyads and Discussion

Directions:

Talk with the children about how communication involves two functions: 1) giving, and 2) receiving messages. We give messages by speaking, and we receive them by listening. In order to be effective communicators, we have to perform both functions well.

Explain: *Let's see how good we are at receiving messages. I have an activity in mind that will give us a chance to see how well we can listen. The activity is called, "Tape the Message and Play It Back." You will try to "tape record" in your mind what someone says, and then tell that person what you heard, to see if you got it right.*

Ask the children to form dyads, and have them decide who is A and who is B. Then direct them through this process:

First minute: A speaks. Topic: *What I Like About My Favorite Game*
Second minute: B "plays back" what he or she heard A say.
Third minute: A compliments B and/or makes corrections.
Fourth minute: B speaks. Same topic, or a new one you choose.
Fifth minute: A "plays back" what he or she heard B say.
Sixth minute: B compliments A and/or makes corrections.

If the children would like to repeat the activity, ask them to change partners. Then guide them through the same process, creating your own topics.

Discussion Questions:

Ask the children:
— *How did you feel when you listened like a tape recorder?*
— *How did you feel when you were the speaker, and were listened to so well?*
— *How did you know you were listened to?*
— *What did you do that helped you be a good listener?*

Other Things To Try:

Suggest that the children try listening very carefully to other people, letting them know they are being heard by repeating back to them some of the things they say. Suggest that they use lead-ins like this: *I believe I really heard you, Mom. You said that . . .*

SOCIAL SKILLS ACTIVITIES FOR THE ELEMENTARY GRADES: Communicating Effectively

Speak Up, Speak Clearly!

Skits and Discussion

Materials:

Copies of *Communication Scenarios* (one copy per group). The Experience Sheets entitled, *Can you Say It Better?* (one per child).

Directions:

Begin by talking with the children in a general way about how much people depend on their ability to communicate with each other. Mention how communication is one of those things that can be very good or very bad. Bad communication causes misunderstandings and other problems. Bad communication can result from unclear communication, or no communication at all. Give examples of unclear or noncommunication, and ask the children how each could create misunderstandings. Ask for examples from the children as well.

As a way to help the children to start thinking, distribute the Experience Sheets, and tell the children that you'd like them to fill in the speech bubbles of the cartoon characters on their own. Read the descriptions of the two situations, and allow some time for the children to fill in the blanks on their sheets.

After they have filled in their Experience Sheets, have the children form small groups. Tell them that they are now going to act out some situations involving communication.

Explain: *I'd like each group to plan and rehearse two short skits. In the first skit, act out the situation the way it is written, showing how poor communication caused problems. In the second skit, using the same basic scenarios, have the characters communicate better, so that no problems occur. Each skit should be 1 - 3 minutes long. Depending on the total number of children, different groups may act out the same skit.*

Continued on Next Page . . .

Speak Up, Speak Clearly!

Skits and Discussion

(Continued)

Give the children time to plan and rehearse their skits. Then ask them to perform for the total group.

Discussion Questions:

At the end of each small group's second skit, ask the children:
— *Do any of these situations remind you of times when you were involved in a misunderstanding? What happened?*
— *Why is it important to communicate clearly and completely?*
— *What can you do to better understand someone who doesn't communicate completely or clearly?*
— *What can you do to make sure you communicate well?*

Communication Scenarios

Unclear Communication:

— Your friend has an argument with his big sister and comes to school in a bad mood. When you see him, he doesn't want to talk and says he wants to eat lunch alone when you invite him to join you. You wonder if you did something to make him upset with you.

— Your parent calls you "an exceptional child" in front of company. You don't know just what your parent means or whether to be pleased or embarrassed by the comment.

No Communication:

— You and your friends plan a party. Everyone says that he or she will bring something either to eat or to drink. You all show up with things to eat, but nobody brings anything to drink. You each blame the others for not planning better.

— You have an argument with a friend and decide to write a note saying you are sorry. Your friend gets the note but doesn't respond. You don't know if your friend is still upset or accepts your apology.

Can You Say It Better

Experience Sheet

Here are two situations in which kids are not communicating well. Read each one. Then follow the directions — *and help them communicate better!*

Situation 1: Randy and Sue like each other, but both are a little shy. Sue just got a new haircut, and Randy thinks it's cute. When she looks at him, he says, "Hey, your hair is short and it's too neat!" He sticks his fingers in her hair and messes it up. The other kids laugh. Sue moves away quickly. She thinks to herself, "I guess Randy doesn't like my new haircut, and he doesn't seem to like me anymore either."

What could Randy say instead? What could Sue say to him? Fill in the bubbles.

Situation 2: Bill and Bud are pals. They decide to go on a five mile hike to the top of a big hill. They agree to meet at the one mile point. Bill says, "It's going to be great! I'll bring some stuff." Bud says, "Yeah, that's good. So will I." They meet at the right place at the right time, but each boy has a blanket and a snake bite kit. Neither has food or water, and they are already hungry and thirsty.

What could Bill and Bud say to each other to make a better plan? Fill in the bubbles.

Being Responsible

We all have responsibilities, and are accountable for our behaviors at home and work alike. Children need to develop responsible behavior patterns in order to take charge of their own lives. They need to learn that being accountable means taking credit—and blame—for their actions. The activities in this unit will help children become aware of ways in which they are (or can become) responsible. In addition, the children will explore and rehearse ways to demonstrate their trustworthiness.

A Way in Which I'm Responsible

A Sharing Circle

Directions:

Introduce the topic: *The topic for today's Sharing Circle is, "A Way in Which I'm Responsible."*

Elaborate: *Think of a responsibility that you accept and carry out. It may be a chore that you do each week, like sweeping the kitchen floor or watering the lawn. Perhaps your responsibility is to do your homework every evening after dinner, or to read a half hour each night before bed. Maybe you get up on time every morning, or fix breakfast for yourself and your younger brothers or sisters. Do you earn and save money? That is a way of being responsible. Before we begin, think quietly for a few moments about something you do that is responsible. The topic is, "A Way in Which I'm Responsible."*

Give each child an opportunity to speak. Listen carefully and encourage the other children to listen too. Thank each one for sharing, and remember to take a turn yourself.

Discussion Questions:

After the sharing in the circle is completed, ask the children:
— *Do we all have a way in which we are responsible?*
— *What did you learn by listening to what other children do that is responsible?*
— *Why do you think it is important to have responsibilities?*

I Admitted That I Did It

A Sharing Circle

Directions:

Introduce the topic: The topic for our circle today is, "I Admitted That I Did It."

Elaborate: Can you think of a time that you did something—either good or bad—and then admitted that you did it? Maybe it was something accidental, like breaking a glass at a friend's house. Or perhaps it was something that you were ashamed of, like taking money from your mom's purse. Maybe it was something that you were proud of, but a little shy about admitting. For example, you might have baked fancy cookies for a class party at school, but felt too embarrassed to tell anyone that you made them. Whatever it was that you did, you took responsibility for it and admitted that you did it—even though it might have taken a lot of courage.

Let's think about it quietly for a minute before we share. The topic is, "I Admitted That I Did It."

Let the children take turns speaking. Encourage them to listen carefully while each child speaks. Thank each child for his or her contribution, and don't forget to share yourself.

Discussion Questions:

After each child who wants to speak has done so, ask some key questions:
— Why is it sometimes difficult to take responsibility for the things we do—whether bad or good?
— Why do you think it is important to take responsibility for what we do?

Trust Walk

Activity and Discussion

You Will Need:

A large room or outdoor area that offers a variety of shapes, textures, and objects for the children to explore, by touch. Blindfolds, such as scarves, dish towels, or pieces of cloth.

Directions:

Explain to the children that this is an activity in which partners work together to build trust. Tell them: *One partner will be blindfolded and the other will be the guide. When you are the guide, lead your "blind" partner around the room or outdoor area safely and carefully, while providing opportunities for him or her to touch different objects, listen to sounds, and smell various aromas.* <u>Don't talk during the activity.</u> *At the end of 10 minutes, I'll give a signal and you will change places with your partner. After 10 more minutes, I will signal you to return to the group to share what happened on your Trust Walk.*

Have the children choose partners. Tell them to decide who will be the guide and who will be the blindfolded person during the first round. Stress the responsibility of the guides to provide a lot of experiences for their partners—but in safe ways. Also remind the children that they may not talk during the exercise. Suggest that they agree on *how* the guide will lead the partner; for example, by holding hands or by linking arms. They may establish *non-verbal* signals to indicate left, right, up, down, fast, or slow.

Discussion Questions:

After each partner has had a turn to be both a blindfolded person and a guide, gather the children together for a discussion and debrief of their experiences. Ask them these questions:

— *What were some of the things you experienced on your walk?*
— *How did you feel being the guide?*
— *How did you feel being guided?*
— *What was it like to do the activity in silence?*
— *What did you learn about being responsible?*

Be Eggs-tra Careful!

Activity and Discussion

Materials:

Raw eggs (one per child), and colored magic markers.

Directions:

Tell the children that they are going to have the responsibility of taking care of something very fragile and delicate for one whole day. They will be given a raw egg to take with them everywhere they go for the next twenty-four hours.

Give each child a raw egg. Tell the children to decorate the eggs with magic markers, making sure not to break them. Have them name their eggs, and treat them like special friends. If you like, break an egg on a plate or in a bowl, to help the children see how "heartbroken" an egg becomes when it is not properly cared for.

Say to the children: *You must take your raw egg with you everywhere you go for the next twenty-four hours. You may set it on the table while you eat or put it on the nightstand while you sleep, but you may not hide it. It is your responsibility to protect your egg from harm and keep it company. Bring it back next time we meet, to show that you kept it safe.*

Discussion Questions:

The next time you meet, lead a discussion of the experiences the children had protecting their eggs. Ask them:
— *What did you do to protect your egg during your daily activities?*
— *What did you say to other people about your egg?*
— *Did you have any "close calls," or did you let your egg get broken?*
— *How did you feel about being in charge of something so fragile for a whole day?*
— *What did you learn about being responsible while doing this activity?*

Critter Talk

Creative Role Play

Materials:

Chalkboard and chalk, or butcher paper and magic markers.

Directions:

In this activity, the children will assume the role of their pet, in order to understand the animal's perspective. Begin by brainstorming the kinds of pets that the children have or would like to have. List them on the board or butcher paper. Then discuss the care that each animal would require in order to stay healthy and happy. Be sure to include exercise, shelter, food and water, companionship, affection, pest control, and cleanliness. This will bring to awareness the needs of each kind of animal, so that the children can more easily role play their chosen animal.

Ask the children to think about their own pet—or the pet they would like to have. Say to them: Now that *we have listed various kinds of pets, and the care each needs to survive and be happy, put yourself in the place of that animal and think about what it would say about you if it could talk. What would your pet turtle, Horace, say about how you care for him? Would your dog, Fluffy, say that you take her for a run every morning and evening? Do you think your guinea pig, Grover, would brag about how clean you keep his cage? Pretend you are your pet and talk with a partner who is taking the role of his or her pet.*

Ask volunteers to come before the group, two or three at a time, to role play their pets in an animal "chit chat." Encourage them to say what their animals would *really* say if they could talk. Suggest that they assume the mannerisms of the animals, but focus on how their owner or master takes care of them. Allow 1 1/2 to 2 minutes per scenario.

Discussion Questions:

After the role play, ask the children:
— *In what ways did you become more aware of the needs of your animal when you took its role?*
— *What would happen to your pet if you were not responsible in caring for it?*
— *How is having a pet a big responsibility?*

One of My Responsibilities

Art Activity

Materials:

Newsprint or art paper, pencils, black construction paper, white glue, colored chalk, facial tissues, and hair spray.

Directions:

This activity can be used right after the Sharing Circle topic, *A Way in Which I Am Responsible.*

Place the materials on a table or workspace. Tell the children that they are going to draw one of their responsibilities with glue on black paper. After the glue dries, they will fill in the spaces with colored chalk.

Explain: *Think of one of the ways in which you are responsible and draw it with pencil on the newsprint. It may be something you shared in the Sharing Circle, or some other responsibility. For example, you might want to draw your hand holding a dog's water dish under a faucet—or yourself getting up on time in the morning. Experiment by drawing a variety of sketches. Keep your objects big and simple. When you are satisfied with a sketch, draw it on the black paper. Use the white glue to go over the pencil lines.*

Collect the drawings. Let the glue dry for several hours or overnight; it will be transparent when dry. Tell the children to fill in the shapes with colored chalk, using only one finger to spread the chalk evenly. They can clean the finger with a tissue as they change chalk colors, and wash their hands when they are done. Seal the pictures with a light coating of hair spray to keep the chalk from smearing.

Discussion: As the children work, talk about those responsibilities that they consider the most important. Ask them how they feel about what their pictures depict. Display the completed pictures around the room before sending them home with the children.

An Interview With a Parent

Experience Sheet

Take this sheet home and interview your parent or guardian about his or her responsibilities. Then bring it back and share your findings with the rest of the group.

Person being interviewed: _____

Interviewer: _____

What is an important responsibility that you have at work (or home)?

Answer: _____
_____

What do you think are your most difficult responsibilities as a parent?

Answer: _____
_____

In what ways are you rewarded for being responsible?

Answer: _____
_____

Do you have any responsibilities that are fun? What are they?

Answer: _____
_____

What responsibilities did you have when you were my age?

Answer: _____
_____

How can I be more responsible at home?

Answer: _____
_____

Following Rules

Every place we go has rules and standards we are expected to follow. Generally, these rules help protect us from harm. For example, speed limits keep us safer on the road. Other rules help maintain order and protect our rights and the rights of others. Knowing how and why such rules exist usually makes children more willing to follow them. This unit will help children understand what rules are, and how they make systems, games, and our lives function better.

A School Rule I Appreciate

A Sharing Circle

Directions:

Introduce the topic: *Our topic for today is, "A School Rule I Appreciate."*

Elaborate: *Sometimes we take rules for granted. We don't stop to think what would happen if we didn't have rules to guide our behavior. Think about all the different kinds of rules you have at your school, and tell us one that you appreciate. It can be a classroom rule, or a playground rule, or a rule that is for the school in general. In deciding, consider the ways you benefit from the different rules. Perhaps you're happy there is a "no hitting" rule because you are small. Or maybe you appreciate a "taking-turns" rule because you are shy and wouldn't get a turn without such a rule. Think about it for a few moments. The topic is, "A School Rule I Appreciate."*

Invite the children to take turns speaking. Listen carefully to each one and encourage the other children to do the same. Allow no negative interruptions. Make sure you share too.

Discussion Questions:

After everyone who wants to speak has done so, ask the children:
— What rules were mentioned most often?
— Why do you think they were mentioned more than others?
— How do rules make things go more smoothly?
— What do you think would happen if there were no rules?

Something I Did to Improve Our Environment

A Sharing Circle

Directions

Introduce the topic: *Our topic for this session is, "Something I Did to Improve Our Environment."*

Elaborate: *Think of a time when you did something to improve your surroundings. It could have been picking up trash in your yard or on the school grounds, or painting over graffiti on a wall. It could have been planting a tree, pulling weeds, taking out the trash, or painting a mural on a blank wall. Improving the environment can involve either cleaning up an area, or making an area more beautiful by adding something to it. Take a few moments to think of a time when you made an improvement in one of these ways. The topic is, "Something I Did to Improve Our Environment."*

Invite the children to share. Listen carefully and encourage the other children to do the same. Thank each child who shares. Remember to take a turn yourself.

Discussion Questions:

After everyone who wants to speak has done so, ask the children:
— Which is more fun, cleaning up an area, or adding something to beautify it? Why?
— What do you think would happen if we didn't do things to keep our environment clean?
— What are some areas you know of that could be made more attractive?

If I Ruled the World . . .

Fantasy/Group Activity

Materials:

A box containing cards or slips of paper, each with a different rule written on it. (Examples are: "Trash must not be thrown out of car windows." "People may not possess illegal drugs.") Paper and pens.

Directions:

Introduce the activity by asking the children: *Why do we have rules or laws? Are they really necessary?*

Have a volunteer pull a card and read the rule on it. Ask, *What's one possible reason for this rule?* or *Why would someone have made this rule?* Lead a discussion about the importance of rules.

Have the children form groups of three or four. Tell them that each group is going to create an imaginary land, and establish a set of rules for the people who live there.

Explain: *Give your land a name, agree on what it is like, and decide who can live there. Then establish a set of rules, and decide what will happen to people who don't cooperate with those rules.*

Discussion: As the children are creating their lands, encourage them to look at the "whys" of their rules, and at what would happen if they didn't have such rules.

Ask volunteers to describe their lands and the rules they established for people who live there. Take advantage of this time to discuss and reinforce specific rules that are necessary to maintaining order.

Other Things To Try:

In preparation for the initial discussion, instead of writing rules on cards yourself, have each of the children think of a rule and write it down.

Rules and Rhymes

Poetry/Art Activity

Materials:

Paper, crayons, magic markers, and Shel Silverstein's book, *Where the Sidewalk Ends*.

Directions:

Distribute the materials. Tell the children that each of them is going to have an opportunity to write a poem about one or more rules, and draw a cartoon to illustrate the poem.

Read Shel Silverstein's poem, "Sarah Cynthia Sylvia Stout Would Not Take the Garbage Out," and show the children the illustration that accompanies it. Show them other pages in the book too, so they can see several examples of the simple line cartoons that illustrate the poems. Next, ask the children to think about rules that they would like to make, change, or get rid of. Generate enough discussion to help each child decide on a subject for his or her poem. Tell the children to start the writing/illustrating process.

Discussion: As the children work, talk with them about the rules they picked to be the subjects of their poems. Encourage them to keep their poetry light and humorous. Praise the children for their ideas, rather than for the quality of their writing or art work.

When they are finished, have the children share their poems. Then collect the cartoons and compile a cartoon book.

Other Things To Try:

Have the children make a book of poems and cartoons based on the lands they created in the *If I Ruled the World* activity.

It's All in the Game

Game Creation and Discussion

Materials:

Two boxes, and various objects to place in the boxes (like whistles, balls, sticks, marbles, buttons, tools, etc.), paper, and pens.

Directions:

Introduce the activity by asking the children to think of some games they like to play. Pick two or three of the games they mention, and discuss the rules that govern them.

Divide the children into two groups, Give each group a piece of paper and pen, and a box with some objects in it.

Explain: *Look at the objects in your box. Your task is to create a game with those objects. Decide what rules are necessary in order for the game to work. Are there any penalties for breaking the rules? If so, what are they? Give the game a name, and write the rules on the sheet of paper. Each group will then teach the other group how to play its game, explaining the rules that govern it.*

During the activity, be encouraging. Offer some suggestions if the children really get stuck, but allow them as much independence as possible.

Have each group take a turn teaching its game and rules. Play each game for a short period of time.

Discussion Questions:

After playing both games, talk about each of them. Ask:
— *Would any other rules help make this game more fun?*
— *Were any of the rules unnecessary?*
— *Should any of the rules be changed?*
— *Why is it important for people to follow rules?*
— *What would happen to the game if the players didn't follow the rules? . . . Would the same thing happen in real life if people didn't follow rules?*

Rules Are Rules

Experience Sheet

Think of the many different areas of your life in which you are required to follow the rules. Then answer these questions:

The best rule at home or school is: _____
_____

The worst rule at home or school is: _____
_____

It should be changed because: _____
_____
_____

If I were in charge of the world, here are three rules I would make immediately:

Rule: _____

Reason for rule: _____
_____

Rule: _____

Reason for rule: _____
_____

Rule: _____

Reason for rule: _____
_____

Understanding Body Language

Even the most convincing of words isn't as true an indicator of how someone feels as is that person's body language. Even in silence, body language speaks loudly and eloquently—but it also has the effect of underscoring spoken language. Clearly, words convey only a part of each message. We can tell a great deal about other people by their expressions, gestures, and movements, and those same indicators reveal to others a great deal about us. This unit is designed to help children become more aware of the unspoken messages that they exchange with others on a daily basis.

Someone Didn't Say a Word, But I Knew How He or She Felt

A Sharing Circle

Directions:

Introduce the topic: Our topic for today is, "Someone Didn't Say a Word, But I Knew How He Or She Felt."

Elaborate: We tend to think we communicate with just the words we speak. However, we also give off clear messages *without* saying a word. Or we say words, but our bodies say something very different from our words. Think of a time when someone you know didn't say a word, yet you took one look and knew that person was unhappy or angry or delighted or scared. Describe how you think the person felt, and what it was about how the person looked that communicated his or her feelings so clearly. Take a few moments to think it over. The topic is, "Someone Didn't Say a Word, But I Knew How He Or She Felt."

Invite the children to take turns speaking. Listen carefully and encourage the other members of the circle to do the same. Thank each child, and remember to take a turn yourself.

Discussion Questions:

After everyone who wants to speak has done so, ask the children:
— How were you able to tell what the person was feeling without being told?
— What were the most obvious clues to the person's feelings?
— If you didn't know someone, do you think you could tell how that person was feeling? Why or why not?

I Didn't Say a Word, But They Knew How I Felt

A Sharing Circle

Directions:

Introduce the topic: *Our topic for today is, "I Didn't Say a Word, But They Knew How I Felt."*

Elaborate: *In the last circle, we talked about being able to determine the feelings of others without their telling us. In this circle, think of a time when another person, or a group of people, knew how you were feeling, even though you didn't tell them. Maybe you were disappointed, joyful, embarrassed, confused, angry, or thrilled. Whatever the feeling was, someone could see it in you, and told you so. Take a few minutes to think of such a time. The topic is, "I Didn't Say a Word, But They Knew How I Felt."*

Invite the children to take turns speaking. Listen intently and thank each child who shares. Don't allow any negative interruptions. Be sure to take a turn yourself.

Discussion Questions:

After everyone who wants to speak has done so, ask the children:
— *Was it OK, or were you uncomfortable knowing that others could tell how you were feeling?*
— *How do you think the others knew what you were feeling?*
— *What was good about someone's being able to figure out how you felt?*

SOCIAL SKILLS ACTIVITIES FOR THE ELEMENTARY GRADES: Understanding Body Language

That's a Fine "How-Do-Ya-Do"

Verbal/Nonverbal Experiment and Discussion

You Will Need:

Cassette recorder; upbeat musical tapes; an unobstructed, open space; and a watch or clock for timing.

Directions:

Set the recorder up in an area where it will not be in the way of moving children. Play the music throughout the activity.

Explain: *Mill around the room and greet as many people as you can in five minutes. Try to use different words and methods to greet each person. It's OK to say something someone else has said, but you must not use the same greeting twice.*

Tell the children to begin. Call time at the end of five minutes.

Explain: *Mill around and greet everyone again, but this time do it nonverbally. You may use gestures, movements, facial expressions, even sounds, but you may not use words! Again, it is OK to do something that someone else has done, but don't use the same method twice. Greet everyone in the group differently.*

Tell the children to begin, and call time at the end of five minutes.

Discussion Questions:

At the end of the experiment, call the children together and ask:
— How did you feel when you couldn't use words?
— What are some nonverbal greetings you used that you had never thought of before?
— What similarities did your greetings have?
— Which method did you think was most effective—verbal or nonverbal?
— Even when no words we're used, could you tell what the other person was communicating to you?

Let Your Feelings Be Your Guide!

Movement/Observation Activity

Materials:

A list of situations, each of which generates a different emotion or reaction. For example, "Your teacher just caught you looking on someone else's test paper;" "Your mom just said you can have a puppy;" "You just broke your favorite CD or cassette;" "You are home alone and you hear strange noises outside your bedroom window;" "Your little sister or brother has been fooling around in your room;" "You have just been given a good citizenship award from the school principal."

Directions:

Ask the children to form a circle. Have them extend their arms outward and touch each other's outstretched hands. This will allow plenty of space for movement.

Explain: *When I call out a situation, you must respond nonverbally in a way that seems appropriate to that situation. For example, if I say, "You have just won the lottery," you might do this:* (Demonstrate by jumping up and down, waving your arms, or letting your mouth drop open). *Now show me how you would respond to the lottery example. While you are reacting, notice the reactions of others too.*

Encourage the children to really "get into it."

Call out another situation such as, "Your best friend just moved to another city." Allow enough time for the children to respond. Remind them to respond nonverbally, and to look around and make mental note of the different ways in which the other children respond.

Continued on Next Page . . .

SOCIAL SKILLS ACTIVITIES FOR THE ELEMENTARY GRADES: Understanding Body Language

Let Your Feelings Be Your Guide!

Movement/Observation Activity

Continue calling out situations until you have exhausted your list.

Discussion Questions:

Generate a discussion by asking these and other questions:
— What kinds of actions or gestures were used for positive reactions? For negative reactions?
— Can you recall seeing someone react differently than you did to the same situation?
— What did you notice about people's facial expressions?
— What have you learned about communication from this activity?
— Do you always need words to communicate what you're feeling, or to understand what someone else is feeling? . . . Explain.

Other Things To Try:

Have the children create and call out situations, or simply <u>feelings</u> that can be expressed nonverbally.

Take It From the Back

Role Play and Observation

Materials:

Three boxes or other containers. In the first box, place approximately 15 slips of paper on which you have written the names of **emotions** or moods, such as mad, sad, furious, irate, happy, etc. (It's OK to repeat emotions, but include as many different ones as you can.) In the second box, place approximately 10 slips of paper on which you have written **body parts**, such as arms, shoulders, feet, and head. (These too can be repeated.) In the third box, place about 5 slips of paper on which you have written different **roles**, such as teacher, parent, coach, or bus driver.

Directions:

Gather the children together and tell them: *Today you are going to have a chance to do some role playing, but you are not going to use any words. You will use only your body to get the message across. And when it's your turn to take part in a role play, you'll do it with your back to the rest of us. We will try to guess what emotion you are acting out.*

Choose two or three volunteers for the first role play. Have them silently draw one slip from the emotion box, turn their backs to the group, and independently (and nonverbally) act out the emotion they've drawn. Ask the group to guess what emotion is being dramatized. Ask for new volunteers and do two or three more rounds like this one.

Next, have the players draw both an emotion *and* a body part. This time when they turn their backs to the group, they must act out the emotion using *only that one body part*. Do three or four rounds in this manner, with the large group guessing the emotion.

Continued on Next Page . . .

Take It From the Back

(Continued)

Role Play and Observation

Finally, have the players draw both an emotion and a role; for example, "mad" and "grandmother." Repeat the procedure described above.

Discussion Questions:

Following the activity, generate a discussion by asking these and other questions:
— *Were you surprised that you could correctly identify emotions from the back? . . . from the movement of only one body part?*
— *Which emotions or moods were the toughest to determine?*
— *What were some of the main indicators of anger? fear? sadness? etc.*

Checkin' It Out

Observation and Discussion

Materials:

The Experience Sheet entitled *Take a Close Look!* (one per child).

Directions:

Gather the children together and tell them: *We've done several activities in which we've role played different feelings and situations, observed each other's nonverbal behavior, and tried to figure out what emotions were being expressed. Now we're going to practice our observation skills where we can observe people we <u>don't</u> know expressing <u>real</u> feelings.*

Pass out the Experience Sheet *Take a Close Look!* and ask the students to quietly observe others and to write about what they see on their experience sheets. Remind them that you will discuss what they have observed at the next class meeting.

Discussion Questions:

At the next class session, lead a discussion regarding the children's experiences. Ask them:
— *What kinds of feelings did you observe most often?*
— *Which moods/feelings were easiest to identify?*
— *Are you more aware of body language now than you used to be?*
— *Was it easier to write what you observed, or to draw it?*

SOCIAL SKILLS ACTIVITIES FOR THE ELEMENTARY GRADES: Understanding Body Language

Take a Close Look!

Experience Sheet

If you look closely, you can tell how people feel by the **expressions on their faces**, and by the **way they move their bodies**.

Go to a busy place where you can sit down and watch lots of people go by. **Look closely, and write down what you see.**

Describe a happy person: **Draw a picture here:**

head _____

eyes _____

mouth _____

shoulders/arms _____

hands _____

posture _____

legs/feet _____

Describe an angry person: **Draw a picture here:**

head _____

eyes _____

mouth _____

shoulders/arms _____

hands _____

posture _____

legs/feet _____

Describe a tired person: **Draw a picture here:**

head _____

eyes _____

mouth _____

shoulders/arms _____

hands _____

posture _____

legs/feet _____

Making and Keeping Friends

Cooperation, support, and having fun together are some of the things we experience with our friends. Our network of friends is one of the most important areas in which we develop social awareness. Children learn skills for interacting with others through successful interaction with their peer group. And having friends to care for and rely on can help them cope effectively with life's daily challenges. This unit is designed to help children develop the ability to establish and maintain friendships. The children will explore the responsibilities of being a friend, and learn what behaviors might cause them to lose friends. In addition, they will have the opportunity to experience directly some of the benefits of friendship.

Something I Like About One of My Best Friends

A Sharing Circle

Directions:

Introduce the topic: *The topic for our circle today is, "Something I Like About One of My Best Friends."*

Elaborate: *Most of us have several close friends, or "best" friends. Think about one of the things that you especially like about one of your best friends. Is it how he treats you? Could it be that she walks home from school with you everyday? Perhaps your friend is funny, or helps you with your spelling. Maybe he plays two-square with you at recess. Don't tell us your friend's name, just the special thing that you like about him or her. Let's take a minute to think quietly about it before we share. The topic is, "Something I Like About One of My Best Friends."*

Invite each child to take a turn speaking, while everyone else listens carefully. Be sure to take a turn yourself.

Discussion Questions:

After the sharing, ask the children:
— Were we able to think of one thing that we liked about a friend?
— How were these things alike or different?
— Why is it important to think about what we like in a friend?

Something I Do to Keep a Friend

A Sharing Circle

Directions:

Introduce the topic: *Our topic for today's session is, "Something I Do to Keep a Friend."*

Elaborate: *We all have new friends and old friends. What is it that we do to keep a friend for a long time? Think about one of the things you do to make certain that someone will keep choosing you as his or her friend. Are you kind to him? Do you play ball with her after school? Do you invite him to ride his bike with you to the park on Saturdays? Maybe you help him or her practice the multiplication tables. Perhaps you share your ice cream with her when you buy one. Think quietly about it for a few moments before we start. The topic is, "Something I Do to Keep a Friend."*

Invite the children to take turns speaking, and encourage them to listen to each other carefully. Be sure to take a turn yourself.

Discussion Questions:

After each child has had a chance to speak, ask the children:
— Were we all able to think of something that we do to keep a friend?
— How were these things alike and different?
— Why is it helpful for us to think of something that we do to keep a friend?

Friends Support Each Other

A Cooperative Game

You Will Need:

An outdoor space, free of glass, rocks, or holes; or an indoor space with mats or carpeting.

Directions:

Brainstorm with the children ways in which friends give each other support. Include suggestions such as, "encouraging friends to do their best in a ball game or race," "helping friends with chores or homework," and "sharing P.E. equipment." Also include "listening to friends when they have important things to say," "sharing feelings," and "consoling friends when they are upset." Discuss with the children how they feel when supported by *their* friends in these ways.

Tell the children that they are going to play a game in which they give each other physical support. It is a fun game in which friends may end up struggling, stumbling, and giggling, as well as supporting each other. They will start with one partner, and add another each time they accomplish their task. Say to them: *You will begin the game by sitting on the ground, back-to-back with your partner, knees bent and elbows linked. All you have to do is stand up together. With a little practice and cooperation, it will be pretty easy.*

After the partners have mastered standing up back-to-back, have some of them divide and join other partners to make groups of three, with the same task. Then try groups of four, five, and so on. A whole group stand-up can be achieved by having everyone sit close and stand up quickly, at exactly the same moment.

Expect a lot of giggling and falling over. Don't be concerned if the large group stand-up doesn't work. The fun is in the trying.

Discussion Questions:

After groups of various numbers have made several attempts to stand up, gather the children together and talk about how they felt when they were able to stand up together. Ask them:
— *How did it feel to support each other, and cooperate with one another?*
— *Was it easy to do every time?*

Putting Your Best Side Forward

Art, Brainstorm, and Discussion

Materials:

Large pieces of butcher paper, masking tape, scissors, and marking pens in assorted colors.

Directions:

Divide the children into several small groups of about six children each. Give each group a piece of butcher paper and markers and scissors. Have one child in each group lie down on the butcher paper and the others trace around that child's body with a marking pen to make a "person shape." When the tracing is finished, the person shape should be cut out. On one side of the person's head have the children draw a happy face and on the other side draw a sad face.

Explain to the children that you want each small group to brainstorm qualities that they value in a friend. These might include honesty, helpfulness, friendliness, and being a good listener. When they think of a positive quality they are to write it on the happy face side.

Then tell the children that you want them to also think of qualities that they wouldn't like in a friend such as lying, tattling, name calling and putting others down. Write these on the sad face side. Ask them to try to fill up both sides with plenty of descriptions. Circulate and offer help as the groups brainstorm and fill up their people shapes.

When the children finish, have each group share both sides of its completed drawing with the entire class. Display the completed people shapes in the room with the positive sides showing.

Discussion Questions:

After each role play, ask the children:
— *Which qualities came up in all groups?*
— *What ideas did you get about friendship that you hadn't thought of before?*
— *How can you use something you learned from this activity in your own friendships?*

String Painting With a Partner

Art Activity

Materials:

White construction paper, one 2-foot piece of string per child, and tempera paint in several colors.

Directions:

Tell the children that each of them, along with a partner, is going to participate in a cooperative art activity. Partners can make two paintings so that each child can take home one of them. Before the activity begins, have the children pair up. If there is an extra person, you can be his/her partner.

Place the materials on large workspaces. Have each pair decide on two colors for its string painting. Contrasting colors, such as red and blue, or a light and dark color, work best. Tell the children: *First, fold your drawing paper in half. Then reopen it. One of you will dip your string into a color of paint, holding onto one end of the string. Carefully place the painted string on one half of the paper, creating some kind of a design. Keep holding the dry end of the string, and let it stick out of the paper, while your partner folds the other half of the paper over the string. Your partner will then press lightly with his or her hands on the outside of the paper while you pull out the string. Open the paper. Next, your partner will repeat the process with his or her string, using another color of paint, and will make a design over yours while you press on the paper.*

The result will be a beautiful two-color butterfly, with one color underneath the other. Let each team make two paintings. Be sure to allow time for clean up.

Discussion: As the children work, ask them how they feel about creating a piece of art as a team. *Do they need to have some special talent to do this? Do they need to cooperate to accomplish the task? Is it fun?* Have the partners share their paintings with the group.

Other Things To Try:

See if the partners would like to "dance" their paintings. Have them notice how the two colors relate to each other on the paper. What shapes and directions do they take? Play some music and let the partners choreograph their string paintings.

My Circle of Friends

Experience Sheet

1. Write the names of your friends on the lines provided around this "Circle of Friends."

2. Use magic markers or colored pencils to draw yourself on the figure without a face. Add your name to that line.

3. Draw a circle around each word that describes a good friend. Then draw a line connecting each circled word with a friend that the word describes. It's OK to connect the same word to more than one friend. You will probably end up with lines criss-crossing each other all over the circle!

IMPORTANT: This sheet is private. Take it home and fill it out. Keep it for yourself, so that you can think about your friends and what their friendship means to you. You don't have to show it to anyone, if you don't want to.

Cooperating With Others

No person can be completely independent within a group, no matter how large or small the group is. Cooperation is necessary for a group to achieve a goal, perform a task—or even continue to exist. And every member of a group is dependent upon other members for support. Knowing how to cooperate with others is a valuable social skill. This unit is designed to help the children learn to understand the dynamics of interdependence by participating in cooperative group endeavors. The children will experience the fun and satisfaction of participating in successful group enterprises, and—perhaps—the disappointment that results when someone in the group lets everyone else down.

A Time I Came Through for the Group

A Sharing Circle

Directions:

Introduce the topic: *The topic for today is, "A Time I Came Through for the Group."*

Elaborate: *We are all members of several groups; for example, families, classes at school, clubs, and perhaps baseball or soccer teams. Can you think of a time when you did something that really helped one of your groups? Maybe you helped your class win an attendance banner by coming to school one day when you didn't feel well. Or perhaps you made a good pass that resulted in a goal for your soccer team. Did you ever run to the store for milk or something else that your family needed for dinner? Perhaps you memorized the Cub Scout Promise so that your den could win a prize for having learned it first. Think quietly about it for a few moments before we begin to share. The topic is, "A Time I Came Through for the Group."*

Give each child an opportunity to speak. Listen carefully and encourage the other children to listen too. Thank each child for sharing, and remember to take a turn yourself.

Discussion Questions:

After the sharing in the circle is completed, ask the children:
— How did you feel about coming through for a group?
— How do you think the other members of the group felt?
— Why do you think it is important for everyone in a group to pull together and cooperate?

A Time Someone Ruined It for Everyone

A Sharing Circle

Directions:

Introduce the topic: *Today the topic for our circle session is, "A Time Someone Ruined It for Everyone."*

Elaborate: *Have you ever been with a group when someone did something to ruin the experience for everyone else? Maybe someone in your class shouted out when you were lining up for recess, and the whole class had to stay inside for an extra five minutes. Perhaps someone ruined a birthday party by starting a fight over the biggest piece of cake. Have you ever been to a family outing at which someone started crying or throwing a tantrum, so you all had to go home? Don't mention any names, but tell what the person did to spoil the event for everyone else. Let's quietly give it some thought for a minute. The topic is, "A Time Someone Ruined It for Everyone."*

Let the children take turns speaking. Encourage them to listen carefully while each child speaks. Thank each child for his or her contribution, and don't forget to share yourself.

Discussion Questions:

When the circle session is finished, summarize by asking:
— How did you feel when someone ruined it for everyone else?
— Why is it important to remember that one person's behavior can affect the whole group?

People Pyramids

Cooperative Stunts

You Will Need:

An open space with tumbling mats, or a grassy area free from holes, rocks, and glass. A camera with film.

Directions:

Explain to the children that they will be building pyramids with their own bodies. Point out that every person is important to the support and shape of the pyramid.

Divide the children into groups of six for the first pyramid. For safety, make sure they are wearing soft-soled shoes, or have them take off their shoes. Have the three huskiest children in each group line up shoulder-to-shoulder on their hands and knees, keeping their backs straight. Have two mid-sized children carefully climb onto the lower children, each mid-sized child straddling two husky ones. Tell the mid-sized children to place their hands on the shoulders of the lower children, and their knees (and shins) on the lower backs. Top the pyramid off with a "lightweight." Take a picture of the people pyramids so the children can see themselves.

When the children are ready to "break up" their pyramids, have them collapse and roll toward the outside—all at the same time. This is safer than having them try to climb down from the pyramid. However, be prepared for laughter and squeals.

Variations: Try making a castle, by creating a circular base, with the children facing inward. The children on the upper levels will also face inward. Ask each group of children to plan another kind of pyramid, exploring directions and shapes, and then build it.

Discussion Questions:

After the children have finished the stunts, ask them:
— *How did you feel about building a pyramid with your group?*
— *Why do you think it is important for each member of the group to support the others?*

Sponge Painting With My Group

Cooperative Art Activity

Materials:

Large pieces of butcher paper; white construction paper; tempera paints poured into pie tins; sponges cut in half, or quartered.

Directions:

Tell the children that they are going to create an imaginary machine with gears, wheels, and other machine parts. They will work cooperatively in groups to complete the project, but each person's contribution will be unique.

Divide the children into groups of six to eight. Give each group a large piece of butcher paper, several colors of paint (with a sponge for each color), and one piece of construction paper per group member. Each person will then tear his or her piece of construction paper into the shape of a machine part such as a wheel, shaft, gear, or belt.

The first person will place his or her paper machine part somewhere on the large piece of butcher paper and sponge paint around the edges by dipping the sponge into one color of paint and dabbing it onto the paper. The next person will place his or her part near the first part, and sponge paint around it so that the parts are connected by paint. Repeat the process until everyone in the group has connected a part to the machine. Go around the group again until the children decide that their machine is finished.

As the children work, watch to see if any groups are having difficulty with the activity. Emphasize the need for group cooperation—and for acceptance of every person's contribution. After the machines are completed, have each group work cooperatively to decide on a name, and describe the function of the

Continued on Next Page . . .

Sponge Painting With My Group

Cooperative Art Activity

Tear paper

Dip sponge into paint

Dab sponge with paint around torn paper

machine. Then have each group present its machine to the others. Hang up the machines for all to see and enjoy.

Discussion Questions:

While the groups are working on their sponge paintings, ask the following questions:
— *Was it easy or difficult to work together as a group? . . . Why?*
— *How did it feel to work as part of a group?*
— *What did you learn from this activity about working cooperatively?*
— *What are things you can do to help your group work well together?*

Let's Skin the Snake

Movement Activity

You Will Need:

A large grassy area, free from holes, stones, or glass—or an open space indoors, with mats.

Directions:

Tell the children that they are going to do a movement activity that will utilize the whole group. It is called "Skin the Snake."

Have the children line up, one behind another. You can use up to 25 in a line. Tell them: *Reach between your legs with your left hand, and grab the right hand of the person behind you. The person in front of you will reach back to grab your right hand, so give it to her. This makes a human chain.* <u>Don't let go.</u> *Now, the last person in line lies down on his back. The person in front of him backs up, straddles his body, and lies down on her back right behind him. By now, the whole group is waddling backwards. Lie down when you are last. The snake has been skinned when everyone is lying down. When the last child to lie down has touched his or her head to the ground, he or she gets up and starts waddling forward again, pulling the rest of the group up and forward until everyone is in the original chain.*

This activity can be turned into a relay between two large teams. The only rule is that if anyone breaks hands during any part of the process, he or she must stop and reconnect before moving again.

During the activity, talk about the need for everyone to cooperate in order to accomplish the task. Laughing is expected, but jeering is not allowed.

Other Things To Try:

Another cooperative movement activity is the "Circle Sit." Everyone stands in a circle, shoulder-to-shoulder. Then everyone turns to the right, and very gently sits down on the knees of the person behind him/her. This is very impressive when done correctly, and very funny when bungled.

A Letter to Me From Five Important People

Experience Sheet

We all depend upon each other in many ways. You need your friends, family, classmates, teachers, and other important people. They need you, too. Here's a letter that the important people in your life can help write *to you*. **Write your name on the greeting line. Then ask five people—children and adults—to each finish one of the sentences in the letter. Have them sign their names at the bottom.**

Dear

I need you for a friend because _____

_____

Something neat that you did for me that I still remember is _____

_____

We had a good time together when we _____

_____

Something that I especially like about you is _____

_____

Something that I'm really glad I did for you was _____

_____

Your friends, _____

_____

_____

_____

_____

Helping Others

Help comes in many forms and from many sources. Sometimes we want help and don't get it; other times we don't want help and we get it anyway. Volunteering our time and talents not only helps others, it creates rewarding experiences for us, and can be a major source of self-esteem. Through helping others, we learn valuable social skills and the benefits of making positive contributions. The formula is a simple one: When we see we've made a difference, we feel good. This unit is designed to help children learn to recognize when help is needed and wanted, how they can lend a hand to one another, and how they can work cooperatively with others to serve the community.

I Helped Someone Who Needed and Wanted My Help

A Sharing Circle

Directions:

Introduce the topic: *The topic for this session is, "I Helped Someone Who Needed and Wanted My Help."*

Elaborate: *Can you think of a time when you helped someone do something? Perhaps the person you helped was struggling to carry some things and you offered to take part of the load. Maybe you helped someone work on a project or a math problem that he or she didn't understand. Or maybe you helped someone finish a job so that the he or she could go somewhere, and, as a result of your assistance, the person was not only able to do the work faster, but better. Take a few moments to think it over. The topic is, "I Helped Someone Who Needed and Wanted My Help."*

Invite the children to take turns speaking. Listen carefully, thank each child, and don't allow negative interruptions. Remember to take a turn yourself.

Discussion Questions:

After every child has had an opportunity to share, ask the children:
— What similarities were there in the things we shared?
— How did you know the person you helped wanted your help?
— How did you feel knowing you helped someone who needed help?

I Got Some Help I Didn't Want

A Sharing Circle

Directions:

Introduce the topic: *Today the topic for our circle is, "I Got Some Help I Didn't Want."*

Elaborate: *Think of a time when you were working on something, and someone came along and started helping you. The problem was, you wanted to do the work by yourself. You didn't want any help. Maybe you were solving a puzzle, completing a school project, or playing a game, and someone tried to tell you how you should do it. You wanted to figure this thing out by yourself, but someone insisted on helping you. Take a moment to think about it before we share. The topic is, "I Got Some Help I Didn't Want."*

Invite everyone to share. You might want to provide an example by sharing first this time. Thank each child for sharing.

Discussion Questions:

When every child in the circle has had a chance to share, ask the children:
— *How did you feel when someone helped, even though you didn't want any help?*
— *Do you think the other people knew their help wasn't wanted?*
— *What could you have said or done to change the situation?*

The Incredible Human Helping Machine

Creative Movement and Problem Solving

Directions:

Divide the children into groups of four or five. Announce that each group will design an *Incredible Human Helping Machine* to "solve" a particular world problem.

Prepare a list of world problems in advance and post them, or allow the groups to brainstorm their own problems. Examples are: abolishing war, eliminating world hunger, eradicating crime, and curing disease. It's OK if more than one group chooses the same problem.

Explain: *Each member of your group will be a machine part, and all of the parts must work together. Each part must move, make a noise, and have a function in the problem-solving. For example, you might be a part that bobs up and down, making a slurping noise as it gobbles up all the nuclear warheads in the world. You must move around, but you cannot get more than an arm's length away from the other parts that make up your machine. Before you start building, get together and decide what problem you want to solve, how your machine will solve the problem, and how each of you will function within the machine that solves it.*

As soon as the machines are all "up and running," have each group explain and demonstrate its machine to the total group. While the machine is working, walk up and touch one member of the group. Tell the children that the part you touched is now <u>malfunctioning</u>. Direct the other members of the group to try to help that part, while continuing their own functioning. Allow them to assist the malfunctioning part for at least 1 minute. If time allows, cause another part of the machine to malfunction.

Continued on Next Page . . .

The Incredible Human Helping Machine

(Continued)

Creative Movement and Problem Solving

Discussion Questions:

Start a culminating discussion using the following questions:
— *What did you learn about helping others from this activity?*
— *What was it like when one part malfunctioned?*
— *As the malfunctioning part, what was it like when others offered help?*
— *As members of a 'Cooperate Machine,' how did you feel about one another?*

All Part of the Warp and Woof

Art Activity

You Will Need:

Magic markers or crayons in a variety of colors; butcher paper pre-cut into strips approximately 4 inches wide and 6 feet long; glue or paste; tables or other large workspaces; cassette recorder and tapes of up-beat music to play throughout the activity (optional).

Directions:

Divide the children into two groups—the Warpers and the Woofers. Pass out the materials. Announce to the children that they are going to create a group weaving. Explain that *warps* are threads or yarns that run lengthwise through a weaving, and that *woofs* are filling threads that run over and under the warps. Tell them that *warp and woof* is also an English-language expression that means *foundation* or *base*.

Explain: *Draw pictures on your strip of paper that express the <u>best things about you.</u> The pictures can tell a story about good things you've accomplished, ways in which you help others, or positive traits that you possess. Have fun. The artistic quality of your drawings is not as important as what they stand for.*

After the children have finished drawing, ask them to show their strips to the group, and explain what their drawings represent. Then move to a large area for the weaving.

Select two 4-inch by 6-foot strips of plain or colored paper to serve as the framing strips for the weaving. Lay them out, six feet apart. Ask one of the Warpers to lay his or her warp between the framing strips, so that the ends of the warp overlap the

Continued on Next Page . . .

All Part of the Warp and Woof

(Continued)

Art Activity

framing strips. Paste the ends of the warp in place. Keep the work flat. Then have the rest of the Warpers paste their warps parallel to the first warp. Allow a few minutes for the paste to dry.

Have the Woofers weave their strips one at a time, over and under the warps. As the children work, point out that some of the drawings are covered up by the strips (and drawings) of other children. Suggest that this is symbolic of the way we help and support one another. Even though our best qualities aren't always visible, they are there—supporting the qualities of others in the group.

When the weaving is finished, hang it up for all to enjoy.

Helping Our Community

A Group Service Project

Materials:

Chart paper and magic markers

Directions:

Remind the children of the concept of community service, and talk with them about some of the kinds of things that they, as young people, can do to help others in the community. When you've generated some interest, suggest that the children brainstorm a list of possible projects, select one to do as a group, and develop a detailed plan for completing it.

Facilitate a brainstorming session. Stimulate creative thinking by adding some ideas yourself. For example, *collecting food to help the homeless; doing yard work for a disabled or elderly person; planting trees; writing letters to terminally ill children; stuffing envelopes for some community organization like Hospice; visiting convalescent homes and reading to the patients; cleaning up the trash in a local park; recycling products and donating the money to a worthy cause.* Follow these rules of brainstorming: Record all of the ideas on chart paper; don't allow evaluative comments (either positive or negative) during the brainstorming; keep the momentum going and get as many ideas down as you can.

Help the children narrow down the list by discussing the pros and cons of each suggestion. This is the time to evaluate. When the list has been pared down to just a few possibilities, select a project by consensus, if possible—by majority vote, if not.

Have the children select a project leader. Step aside and let the leader facilitate the planning of the project.

Continued on Next Page . . .

Helping Our Community

(Continued)

A Group Service Project

From the sidelines, try to ensure that the children set up and follow a workable planning process that includes setting a goal, gathering information (through phone calls, etc.), deciding the specific steps that need to be taken to achieve the goal, appointing individuals to take those steps, and developing an accompanying timeline.

Encourage the children to be solution oriented—to think in terms of how things *can* be done rather than why they *can't* be done. Allow time for additional meetings, as necessary.

Discussion Questions:

When the project has been successfully completed, ask the children:
— *What was the most rewarding aspect of the project for you?*
— *What did you learn from this project that you could use in planning another one?*
— *What did you learn about working together and helping others?*

Extension:

Take photos of the actual project activity, and have the children write reports about their experience. Display the reports and photos around the room. The children can also create a presentation of the project and share it with other classrooms and/or at a parent night.

I'm a Secret Help Pal

Experience Sheet

Choose someone you know, and become his or her "Secret Help Pal" for one week. You'll be like a big brother or sister, and your pal won't even know it! **Think of some things you could do for your Secret Help Pal. Here are a few ideas:**

    Include your pal in some of your activities.
    Help your pal with homework or chores.
    Introduce your pal to some of your friends.

Keep a daily log:

I helped _____ in the following ways:

Monday: _____

_____

Tuesday: _____

_____

Wednesday: _____

_____

Thursday: _____

_____

Friday: _____

_____

Saturday: _____

_____

Sunday: _____

_____

What was the best thing that happened when you were helping your Secret Help Pal?

_____

_____

_____

Appreciating Differences

Everyone is different. People don't need to change to be like anyone else. We all have special qualities that make us who we are, and those special qualities include such things as language, race, religion, and disabilities. This unit is designed to help children realize that appearance is not as important as the type of person we are—and that it's often what others can't see that counts. Special privileges aren't reserved for certain people. No matter who we are, where we live, or what we wear, we deserve as much happiness and as many friends as anyone else.

A Way I Show Respect for Others

A Sharing Circle

Directions:

Introduce the topic: The topic for this Sharing Circle is, "A Way I Show Respect for Others."

Elaborate: There are many ways that we can show respect for other people. Tell us about a way that you frequently use. Maybe you remember to say please and thank you, or try never to interrupt others when they're talking, or hold doors when you go through them so they won't swing back and smack the people behind you. Perhaps you try not to say critical things about others, or maybe you listen respectfully to the opinions of people you disagree with. Tell us what you do that is respectful, and how you learned to do it. Think about it for a few moments. The topic is, "A Way I Show Respect for Others."

Invite each child to take a turn speaking, while everyone else listens carefully, without interrupting. Be sure to take a turn yourself.

Discussion Questions:

After every child who wants to speak has done so, ask the children:
— How do you feel about <u>yourself</u> when you show respect for others?
— If <u>you</u> want to be respected, will showing respect for others help? How?
— Should we show respect for people we don't like? Explain.

A Friend of Mine Who Is Different From Me

A Sharing Circle

Directions:

Introduce the topic: *Today's Sharing Circle topic is, "A Friend of Mine Who Is Different From Me."*

Elaborate: *Think of a friend of yours who is different from you in some important way. Perhaps your friend is of a different race or religion, or is a lot older or younger than you. Maybe your friend would rather read a book while you watch television, or collect aluminum cans while you collect bugs. Do you have a friend who uses a wheelchair, or stutters, or goes to the hospital for dialysis treatments every few days? Don't mention your friend's name, but tell us how he or she is different from you, and what you particularly enjoy about this friendship. Let's think about it for a few moments. The topic is, "A Friend of Mine Who Is Different From Me."*

Invite the children to take turns speaking. Encourage them to listen carefully to each other. Don't allow negative interruptions, and be sure to take a turn yourself.

Discussion Questions:

After each child who wants to speak has done so, ask the children:
— *When a person thinks or talks differently, or looks different, does that make him or her less worthy of respect? Why or why not?*
— *What can we gain by having friends who are different from us?*
— *What would happen if we insisted that all our friends be just like us?*

Walk a Mile in My Moccasins

Experiment, Dyads, and Discussion

Materials:

An extra pair of socks for each child.

Directions:

Have the children form a circle. Explain that they are going to find out what it feels like to walk in someone else's shoes. Tell them to count off by two's. Ask the 2's to remove one shoe and place it in the center of the circle. Tell all of the children to close their eyes. While their eyes are closed, mix up the shoes. Then tell the 1's to reach in and take the first shoe they touch. Tell the children to open their eyes.

Explain: *Find the person whose shoe you have. Put on both of your partner's shoes, while he or she puts on your shoes. If you're not wearing socks, use one of the extra pairs I've provided. If you are wearing socks, but would like to wear an extra pair over your own, that's OK too. Now, take a short walk with your partner and talk about what it's like to wear each other's shoes. If the shoes are too small for you, notice what that feels like, and do the best you can.*

Allow time for the children to walk and talk. Then, still wearing each other's shoes, have the partners sit together and take turns sharing in response to one of the following topics:
- *A Time I Was Misunderstood*
- *I Was Treated Unfairly Because I'm Different*

Tell the children that when it is their turn to listen, they are to be very attentive and do their best to understand their partner's experience. When their partner is finished speaking, they are to say very firmly and warmly, "I understand." Allow about two minutes of sharing per child.

Discussion Questions:

Have the children form a large group and ask:
— *How did you feel when you were wearing your partner's shoes?*
— *Did you learn anything new about your partner?*
— *Why is it important to try to understand each other's experiences and differences?*

Make Mine a Mixed Bouquet!

Art Activity

Materials:

Colored poster paper, magazines containing photos and illustrations of people and flowers (National Geographic and flower catalogs would be excellent), scissors, glue, and magic markers in various colors. A bouquet containing several different kinds of flowers (optional).

Directions:

Begin this activity by talking to the children about the enormous varieties of flowers that are available to grow, or to buy from the florist. Point out that if they were to go to a florist, they could choose a bouquet made up of only one type of flower, or they could choose a mixed bouquet. Talk about the advantages of choosing a mixed bouquet. Mention that the variety of colors, shapes, textures, and scents would be beautiful, interesting, and stimulating to the senses. (If you brought a bouquet of flowers, use it as an example.)

Compare variety in flowers to variety in people. Point out that the different personalities, colors, backgrounds, religions, and talents in people are even more exciting.

Divide the children into groups of three or four, and distribute the materials. Tell the children that each group is going to make two mixed bouquets—one of flowers, and one of people.

Explain: *Look through the magazines, and cut out pictures of different kinds of people, and different kinds of flowers. Find as much variety as you can. On one sheet of poster paper, arrange a collage of the people in the shape of a bouquet. On the other sheet of poster paper, do the same with the flowers, or you may want to*

Continued on Next Page . . .

Make Mine a Mixed Bouquet!

Art Activity

(Continued)

make one bouquet using both people and flowers together. When you have finished your arrangements, glue the pictures down. Use the magic markers to draw a vase, and to attach a stem with leaves to each person or flower. Complete the collages by adding additional decorations with the magic markers.

Discussion: Circulate and talk with the children while they are creating. Ask them to guess where the people in their pictures work and live, and how they think the people would get along if they knew they were all part of the same bouquet. Talk about the richness that results from combining many unique individuals—whether they are people or flowers.

When the collages are done, put them up for all to see. Title the display, "Make Mine a Mixed Bouquet!"

Celebrating Our Differences

Group Discussion

Directions:

Have the children sit in a circle.

On chalk board or chart paper, write these terms: *race, religion, gender, disability, ethnicity, economic level, place of residence, education, values.*

Discuss the meaning of the terms, giving several examples of each. Point out that these are some of the major ways in which people are different. Ask the children:
— *How do people react to these differences in others?*
— *What would the world be like if we were all the same?*
— *How do you feel when you are with someone who is different from you?*
— *If you feel uncomfortable around someone who is different from you, what can you do about it?*
— *How do you feel when someone puts you down because you are different?*

Have the children pair up with the person next to them. Tell them to turn toward each other, without leaving the large circle. Say: *Look at your partner. Notice as many things as you can about your partner that are different from you. Tell your partner one of the things you notice. Listen while he or she tells you how you are different. Then think about the ways in which you and your partner are the same, and take turns describing to your partner one of those similarities.*

Discussion Questions:

Facilitate a discussion by asking the following questions:
— *What did you notice that was the same about you and your partner? What was different?*
— *What are some ways in which people and groups benefit from individual differences?*

Counting on Each Other

Brainstorm and Discussion

Materials:

One copy of the Experience Sheet *Count On Me!* for each student; chalkboard and chalk.

Directions:

Ask the children to help you brainstorm some of the many different ways people count on one another in the classroom and elsewhere. List their ideas on the chalkboard or chart paper. To facilitate, ask such questions as:
— *What do we count on each other for?*
— *What do you count on me for?*
— *What do you count on your parents for?*
— *What do you count on your neighbors for?*
— *What do you count on your best friend for?*

Divide the children into small groups of 8 to 10. Distribute the Experience Sheets. Announce that you want the children to think about the unique qualities, talents and abilities of each person in their group and write down one way in which they count on that person. Tell them to use the list on the board for ideas. Circulate and offer help as needed and make sure what is written is positive.

When the children have finished, ask the groups to share, within their small group, what each wrote about the other. When everyone has shared, conclude with a class discussion.

Discussion Questions:

Ask the following questions:
— *How do you feel knowing that you can count on so many people?*
— *How do we learn to rely on other people?*
— *How do you let others know they can count on you?*
— *How does knowing you can count on someone build trust?*

Count On Me!
Experience Sheet

I can count on _____ to _____
_____.

I can count on _____ to _____
_____.

I can count on _____ to _____
_____.

I can count on _____ to _____
_____.

I can count on _____ to _____
_____.

I can count on _____ to _____
_____.

I can count on _____ to _____
_____.

I can count on _____ to _____
_____.

I can count on _____ to _____
_____.

I can count on _____ to _____
_____.

Managing Conflict

Conflicts are an inevitable, and sometimes threatening, part of life. But there are things that we can do to turn potentially harmful conflicts into situations in which no one is hurt. This unit is designed to provide the children with non-threatening ways to explore various kinds of conflict. It also gives them opportunities to learn and practice some of the many available conflict management strategies—such as "I" messages, sharing, listening, expressing regret, putting off, compromising, negotiating, and channeling negative energy into physical activity.

I Almost Got Into a Fight

A Sharing Circle

Directions:

Introduce the topic: *Our topic for this session is, "I Almost Got Into a Fight!"*

Elaborate: *From time to time each of us has a disagreement or conflict with another person. Sometimes conflicts aren't very serious, and sometimes they are. Can you think of a time when something happened between you and someone else that almost caused you to get into a fight? Maybe you wanted to fight because you were upset. Or maybe the other person tried to start the fight. Perhaps you both felt like fighting, but then, somehow, you settled the problem peacefully. Tell us how the incident happened, and how you felt, but please don't tell us who the other person was. The topic is, "I Almost Got Into a Fight."*

Invite the children to take turns sharing. Listen carefully to each one and guide the other children to do the same. Don't allow negative interruptions. Be sure to take a turn yourself.

Discussion Questions:

After every child who wants to speak has done so, ask the children:
— Is conflict always bad, or can it sometimes lead to good things?
— What were the main ways we kept these disagreements or conflicts from becoming big fights?

How I Used an "I" Message

A Sharing Circle

Note:

This Sharing Circle should not be done until you have led the next activity, *"I" Messages Ease Tense Situations.*

Directions:

Introduce the topic: *Our topic for this session is, "How I Used an 'I' Message."*

Elaborate: *At our last meeting we did some skits involving "I" messages and "you" messages. Our experience sheets also covered "I" and "you" messages. Do you remember the differences between these two types of messages, and how they affect tense situations?* (Discuss, as necessary.) *In this Sharing Circle, we will each have a chance to tell about a time when we tried using an "I" message, and what happened when we did. If you haven't had a chance to use an "I" message yet, tell us about a time when you didn't use one, and how you think things would have turned out if you had. Tell us all about the incident, but don't tell us the names of the other people involved. Our topic is, "How I Used an 'I' Message."*

Invite the children to take turns speaking. Listen carefully to each one and guide the other children to do the same. Don't allow negative interruptions. Be sure to take a turn yourself.

Discussion Questions:

After each child who wants to speak has done so, ask the children:
— *How did our "I" messages affect the people in these situations?*
— *How did using an "I" message make you feel about yourself?*
— *Why do "I" messages tend to lighten up tense situations?*

"I" Messages Ease Tense Situations

Drama and Discussion

Note:

This activity should be followed by the second Sharing Circle in this unit, *How I Used an "I" Message.*

Materials:

The Experience Sheets entitled, *Don't Say "You," Say "I"* (one per child).

Directions:

Begin by telling the children about two different ways that a person can respond to tense situations. A person can say, "You . . .," or a person can say "I . . ." When you start a sentence with the word, *you*, it's a "you" message. When you start a sentence with the word *I*, it's an "I" message. "You" messages often lead to blaming and name calling and can make the other person mad or hurt. They usually make a problem worse. For example: *You just took my bike without asking, you thief!* "I" messages are usually more tactful. For example: *When I discovered my bike was gone, I felt really scared. I want you to ask me before you use it.* "I" messages tell the other person what the problem is, how you feel about it, and what you want, or don't want, to happen.

Distribute the Experience Sheets. Tell the children to fill in the speech bubbles with "I" messages. Encourage the children to talk about what their ideas are for good "I" messages. Offer help and suggestions as needed. When the children have finished the Experience Sheets, tell them they are now going to act out the scenarios on the Experience Sheet. Choose four volunteers to play the parts of the individuals in the two cartoons (two per cartoon).

Continued on Next Page . . .

"I" Messages Ease Tense Situations

Drama and Discussion

(Continued)

Explain: *Plan two short skits. In the first skit, the person who is <u>responding</u> to the situation should get upset and deliver a "you" message to the person who spoke first. Then the two of you should keep up the negative interaction for awhile. In the second skit, the person responding to the situation should try to lighten things up by using an "I" message. We'll see how these two different ways of responding affect the people involved.*

Give the children time to plan and rehearse their skits. Then ask them to perform for the total group.

Discussion Questions:

At the end of <u>each</u> small group's second skit, ask the children:
— What were the effects of the "you" messages that were delivered in these skits?
— What were the effects of the "I" messages that were delivered in these skits?
— What is the benefit of using an "I" message instead of a "you" message?
— Do you think it requires some practice to learn how to use "I" messages when you're upset?
— What can you do to remember to use "I" messages in conflict situations you face in your own life?

Tell the children: *Our next Sharing Circle topic is, "How I Used an 'I' Message." So if some tense situations come up before we meet again, try using an "I" message. Then you can tell us about the situation, and how your "I" message worked.*

Phony Fighting Can Be Fun

Movement and Discussion

Directions:

Begin the activity by leading a brief discussion about the relationship between negative energy and conflict. Point out that conflicts often occur because people develop pent-up energies, and become frustrated when they can't release them. As a group, think of ways people can channel their energy, especially negative energy, through exercise and sports.

Suggest to the children that they do some movement exercises together. Then lead them through the following movements:

Move away from each other so you won't make contact . . . close your eyes and stretch your arms . . . then wave your arms around . . . now kick your legs out . . . in slow motion, walk with your arms swinging and your legs kicking out very far . . . now run in slow motion.

Find a partner . . . now, one of you make some movements while the other copies them . . . do that for awhile . . . now, switch roles.

Now pretend to have a fight . . . one swings at the other . . . that person rebounds and kicks out . . . the other acts like the kick connected and kicks back . . . keep it up for awhile . . . if this makes you feel like laughing, go ahead!

Note: Caution the children that this is just pretend and they are not to make any physical contact.

Discussion Questions:

Use these and other questions to generate a discussion about the experience:
— How did it feel to put your energy into exercising and pretending to fight?
— Why do you think it helps to exercise when we're experiencing negative energy?
— What are some other forms of exercise that might help?

Conflict Management Strategies on Stage

Drama and Discussion

Materials:

A chart showing the following conflict management strategies:
1) Sharing, 2) Listening, 3) Expressing Regret, 4) Putting Off, and 5) Compromising/Negotiating. The following conflict management scenarios, each written on a separate piece of paper:

• Two people are arguing because they both want something. They agree to share the thing they both want. (Strategy: sharing.)

• Person A is mad at person B. Person A calms down after B listens to A respectfully. (Strategy: listening.)

• Person A is upset about something. Person B expresses understanding of A's feelings and tells A that he or she is sorry that A feels so bad. (Strategy: expressing regret.)

• Two people are already feeling irritable when they start to argue about something. They agree not to say any more now, and to settle the problem later, when they both feel better. (Strategy: putting off.)

• A and B want to have different things, but they can only have one thing at a time. They agree to have some of what A wants first; then to have some of what B wants. (Strategies: compromising/negotiating.)

Directions:

Explain to the children that conflicts are an inevitable part of life, but what makes conflicts upsetting is not knowing how to handle them. If you don't know something positive to do, you may end up making matters worse. Review the Conflict Management Strategies on the chart. Give examples and ask the students to describe problems that might be resolved by each strategy.

Continued on Next Page . . .

(Continued)

Conflict Management Strategies on Stage

Drama and Discussion

Give the five pieces of paper with the conflict management scenarios written on them to five children, and ask each to choose a partner. Explain that each pair is to act out its conflict situation, and to demonstrate the management strategy listed.

Give the children time to prepare their skits. Provide assistance, as needed.

Invite the actors to perform their skits. After each skit, ask the audience which strategy was demonstrated, and put a check mark beside it on the chart. Hold a brief discussion regarding each strategy and how well it works in managing conflict.

Don't Say "You," Say "I"

Experience Sheet

Here are two tense situations. In each one, an "I" message could be used to lighten things up. Read each situation. Draw a picture of yourself in the cartoon. Then, using an "I" message, write your response to what the other person is saying.

Situation One: You are walking down the hall. You see the biggest bullies in the school slam your friend up against a wall. Then you hear them call your friend names. You feel terrible and would like to help, but just then your friend looks at you and angrily says . . .

Situation Two: You borrow your older sister's cassette recorder and a couple of tapes, but then the recorder stops running. You know you haven't done anything harmful to it, but when you give it back, she is very upset. She blames you by saying . . .

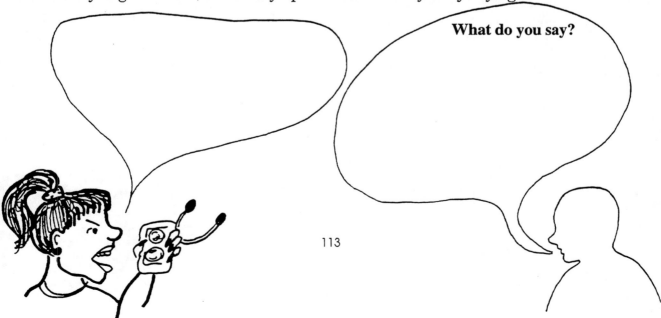